THE BEST IDEA I EVER HAD RIGHT NOW !!!

by Tearod Robertson

TRobertson Publishing, Co.

ISBN (978-0-9888144-0-0)

TABLE OF CONTENTS

FOREWORD

This is my story. This is my song. Whether you like country, gospel, pop or hip- hop music, the beat is the same. The words are the same. One band. One voice. One sound.

My song is one of many ideas that I have acted upon. I have never let The Best Idea I Ever Had Right Now, escape my imagination. I create my dreams, I live my dreams. I have never let anyone steal my dreams. My dreams are the chorus to my song.

Everyone has a story. Everyone has a song. My goal is to share my song with you. My goal will be accomplished if at least one person is able to sample my song, make their song better and make their dreams come true.

The passion I have for life is determined by the passion for my song.

This is my story. This is my song.

CHAPTER 1

IDENTIFYING YOUR DREAMS

The toughest part about starting the business that you have been dreaming about is acting upon creating a plan to really bring it to life. A natural tendency that we like to receive is acceptance with our group of peers.

The first thing we do is share our ideas and thoughts with our peers to get their feedback and hopefully acceptance that our idea is a good one. When, they think that our idea is a joke, we laugh it off as such and never bring it up again. When they ask how we may be able to pull off the idea, we try to come up with some very convincing arguments to reel them in for support. When they think it is a great idea, we take that as confirmation that we are on the path to greatness. This group of peers, I call the World. They are not your peers, they are your World.

I have had people in my World to ask me on many occasions, “What do you really want to do?” They always seem to laugh and smirk at my answer. My reply, I simply want to work for myself. Well it is really not that simple. I want to work for myself, in an office building that I own looking over the Metroplex’s skyline. Now, what exactly do I have to be doing in the building as a business owner? It doesn’t matter. I can be shelling peanuts, operating a t-shirt printing company or running a development business. It truly doesn’t matter. In fact, I guess it really is that simple. I just want to own my own business.

Just like you and the rest of My World, I have Dreams too. It’s just that I have a whole shoebox full of Dreams and, I am making them all come true, one Dream at a time.

Probably the greatest Dreamer of the modern era was Walt Disney. He was fired by a newspaper editor because "he lacked imagination and had no good ideas.” His Disneyland Theme Park was rejected by the City of Anaheim because it was thought not to attract desirable attendees. Go figure.

Remember that is a difference between negative and constructive criticism. Constructive criticism can bring Dreams alive. Negative criticism can kill Dreams. Don't let anyone kill your Dreams.

Regardless of your idea, it is OK to Dream. If you are prepared to accept success, you must also be prepared to accept failure. "Only those who dare to fail greatly can achieve greatly." ~ Robert F. Kennedy

In 1990 I woke up in my first Dream. It was the summer after my freshman year in college. Just as most males would do in that age group (late teens early twenty something), my Dream was being surrounded by the most beautiful women in the World. My Dream was simple I was going to create a calendar of the most beautiful African-American models in the World and sell it.

My concept already had a predecessor. It was the Beauty of the Week center-fold presented in a popular weekly magazine.

I couldn't wait for the magazine to hit the shelves every week. Actually, my parents and grandparents always had paid subscriptions. Every two weeks, the magazine would come in the mail and, I would turn straight to page number forty-three. There she was a scantily clad African-American beauty, wearing a two piece bikini with her basketball rear-end perfectly profiled and her C-cup breast shot dead on by the camera of some lucky guy with a 35mm camera.

The cover of the magazine embraced by a high profiled celebrity, had no bearing on whether or not I would pick it up and thumb thru it. Neither, did the political articles covering the African-American community. It was the model on page number forty-three that had me sold. Thus, I was convinced that a calendar with African-American beauties from January to December would be a big seller to other males who felt that same way I did.

As I conducted my research, I did find that there were other swimsuit calendars out there but, none that were dedicated strictly to women of color. As I shot the idea out there to those in my World, all I kept hearing was how great of an idea it was. At least this is what I received back from those in my World to whom which I shopped the idea. The problem with this was I only shopped the idea to those who looked like me and to those who talked like me. For the most part, I only presented the concept to my friends (who were other African-American males).

This provided a lot of positive feedback. However, all positive feedback with no negative feedback and no constructive criticism is a problem. I had nothing to build my Dream upon. There is no feeling like have what you feel is a great idea and, don't understand how to put it together and make it a reality.

What I began to realize was that I had a good Dream. However, I didn't have a clue of where to start. I lived in a small city that was mostly non African-American and attended a university that had an even less of an African-American population. Thus, I did not have a very big pool to select models for the calendar. I didn't even own a camera to take pictures of models if I did have any. Heck, I didn't even have the money to buy a camera or pay a model. You talk about a good idea, this was it! But, what do you do with an idea that you can't do anything with? Yep, you got it. Find investors.

Well, not really. I shopped the idea to my two best friends, to help me launch it. They were a part of my World that I had initially shopped the idea. There were three of us so we called our bond TRI-SET (SET were the initials of our first names). Of course, they thought the name was pretty cool and, the idea was even cooler. The problem was they had the same resources that I had to make it work. None! But, it was fun talking about it.

It is OK to Dream, however to bring your Dream to life, follow some very basic rules.

Rule #1: Determine if your Dream is worth Pursuing.

Do you have the necessary resources to put your Dream in motion? If your Dream is your passion, you will make it worth pursuing. Nothing will stop you. If you want to design the Kangaroo Pouch (or whatever product you have in mind), ask yourself "Can I sew?" If your answer is yes, then that is great. If your answer is no, then you need to find someone who can, in order to make your mock sample. Do you have some old material lying around the house that you can use to make the sample? If your answer is yes, then great! If your answer is no, then you need to locate a fabric shop that will allow you to purchase a small quantity to make your sample. Once you have your sample piece put together, you are light years ahead of every other person who only has a good idea.

It doesn't matter what your idea is. It doesn't matter if you are trying to create an actual unit of goods or, create a service. You must determine how you are going to get your goods or service to market. There are very few goods or services that an owner can get to market efficiently without having to acquire the assistance of others. The quicker you can determine whose service you will need to take your goods or service to market the quicker you will be able to see your Dream come to life.

Though selling units of a product is what I base most of my business models upon, the same concepts apply to the service industry. For instance, you want to sell your consultation services. OK, place a price on your services and do it. Just understand that if you are selling your Interior Decorating skills as a service, you must ask yourself “Do I have pictures of some of my sample work?” If your answer is yes then great! If no, you need to get busy and start creating sample pieces.

No matter what your Dream is, you must create a sample to bring your Dream to life. A sample gives you credibility that you are well versed in your field of expertise. Very few music artists will get the opportunity to perform on nationally recognized TV shows and become platinum recording artists after a twelve week audition and votes by show viewers.

However a singer who can produce a music track, record it to dat, or adat, drop it to a computer and dub the voice over music can create a sample CD. This same sample can be sent to the major record labels.

Better yet, if the Majors don't have time, the artists can team with the producer, determine a fair revenue split and sell the music online. All of this can be done, with only a sample. Once you have created your sample, you no longer have a Dream. You have a legitimate business.

If you don't have the time or resources to finalize the product of your Dream, create a sample of your Dream, place it in a shoe box and come back to it when you can. No, of course I don't literally mean a shoe box. My shoe box of Dreams and ideas are all in my head. I realize that I am not able to create a sample of them, so I have stored them away on the hard drive in my mind until the opportunity presents itself for me to be able to bring them to life.

The major issue with storing away your Dreams in your shoe box is that if you become mentally impaired or even die, no one will be able to at a minimum realize what about what you were dreaming. I believe that is the primary reason why most Dreamers attempt to share their Dreams as early and as often as they can within their Worlds. Thus, if something does happen to them, at least their World can share with others that the person was a Dreamer.

For Dreamers, new ideas come to your mind when you are least expecting them. You may not be prepared to act upon them as soon as they come to mind. But, you should always be prepared to jot them down. Keep a small pad and pen with you at all times. Or, better yet, input them into the notes of your smart phone. Set aside a specific hour each day to go over your notes and to develop your Dreams or, to just read over your notes. There may be days, weeks, months and even years that you never act upon certain notes. However if it was worth jotting down, one day the topic will come again. It may not become a dream that you build. But, it could become the Dream of someone-else's that your notes could inspire to move forward.

When you set time aside, use this time to create brainstorms. Write down all of the pros and cons of your notes and your ideas. Try to write down at least fifty pros and fifty cons. This will help you to quickly identify which outweigh the other. Just because one out weigh the other, this does not mean that you should or should not pursue building the Dream. This is simply a measuring stick for you to evaluate where the idea really lies in your view of it becoming an actual Dream to begin building.

CHAPTER 2

DREAM BUILDING

The one thing that I have come to realize is that even though one idea may not steer you down millionaire lane it is a great historical reference for future ideas. There is no need to reinvent the wheel every time you come up with your next "best idea you have ever had." Simply, keep notes on things you learned from your last "best idea you ever had." Use the steps that worked for you and discard those things that did not work so well. Eventually, over time you will have a memory drive of mental data that you will be able to apply to your own ventures and share with others as a resident expert on all things entrepreneurial.

Keeping my Dream alive of wanting to create an African-American swimsuit calendar, I introduced the concept to a new friend that I met when I transferred colleges in 1990. That Spring, of 1991, as we spoke about Dreams and aspirations we formed a business partnership. Just as the business relationship I had previously established with my two friends back in my home town and then, we took it a step forward.

Because I already knew what limited resources we had, I was able to share with him some of our earlier setbacks. Fortunately for us, we had a few things that made our potential business situation look a little brighter. First of all, my mother was able to buy me a real nice camera the previous Christmas. The resource of not being able to take pictures of potential models was no longer an issue. My cousin had worked all summer and during the prior school year. He was an artist and had purchased a nice camera as well. So wholla, all of a sudden I was a photographer and I had a freelance photographer on staff as well. We were now well on our way to producing a calendar featuring some of the most beautiful swimsuit models of color that the World had ever seen.

Another resource that we were faced with in my initial phase of attempting to put such a calendar together was the limited number of African-American models who we could solicit to participate in such a project. This resource limitation was eliminated due to the fact that I had transferred colleges. Why does this matter? Yep, you guessed it. I had transferred to a Historically Black College and University in the Heart of Dixie.

Scores of potential African-American models, waiting to be discovered, were everywhere. After-all, this is the same university where Tom Joyner became The Fly Jock, Lionel Richie became a Commodore and the Wynan brothers told their jokes on the "Ignorant Bench." Surely we were destined to be producers of the biggest African-American selling swimsuit calendars with models discovered right there on The Avenue of the university.

We still faced other slight resource issues. That was funding the project. The models had to be paid. There was a cost to have the film developed. We had to purchase the swimsuits for the models to wear. Then we had to pay to have the samples created. We were able to overcome many of the challenges that I had faced while working with my previous friends / business partners. However we were still a long ways away from being able to really produce a calendar. At the time, it seemed as if it was fun to Dream about it but the odds of this really happening were not that great.

That was until every conversation that we had when we saw each other on campus and after class was about the calendar. The more we communicated about the project, the more we realize that the lack of resources would not be a hindrance but a motivation to get the project completed.

We didn't have money to pay the models. But, was money really their motivating factor? After speaking with more than fifty potential models, we came to a realization that money was not necessarily the major motivator. Just as we had a desire to create a calendar of American-American swimsuit models, there were African-American females that had just as big of desires to be models in such calendars. This was their opportunity to potentially gain some national exposure with the hopes of blowing up and becoming a super model.

This was the first of creating many business networking relationships. We began to realize that all Dreams are Compound Dreams. As you dream, someone-else has a dream that will ultimately be affected by the outcome of your dream.

Rule #2: Determine how your Dreams Affect other Dreams

I cannot think of one great successful business that has not greatly influence the success of other businesses.

Let's take a major software developing company for an example. A very smart software programmer creates a program that eighty percent of the World is able to use. In order for him to distribute his software, he has to embed it on a CD. Well, in order to do that he has to do business with a CD manufacturing company to embed the software. The CD manufacturing company has to conduct business with a printing company that will allow it to print labels on its CD. The printing company has to conduct business with ink suppliers. The software developer has to conduct business with the packaging company that makes the boxes in which the software will be boxed in. The packaging company has to conduct business with the paper mills to receive paper products to create the packages. The CD manufacturing company conducts business with manufacturing company that makes the CD jewel case. The CD manufacturing company conducts business with the plastic manufacturer. Each of these entities conducts business with shipping companies to deliver the product to their destinations. Once the final product is completed, boxed and ready to ship, the software developer conducts business with a distributor.

The distributor conducts business with shippers, as well as retailers.

So as you can see, in every business there is no successful business without the success of another. This is indeed for "every" business. Do you want to be a music producer? Then, you need singers, song writers, computers, equipment and etc... Do you want to sell T-Shirts? Then you need an artist for designs, a t-shirt supplier, a screen print machine supplier, a location to sell your T-shirts and etc...

As in the case of our calendar, we identified all of the major players that were needed to get our swimsuit calendar produced. We created a contract for our models. We didn't promise them money. We promised not to use their photos in any demeaning ways. But mostly, we promised exposure. Thus the name of our company became TS Exposure. The T and the S were the initials of our first names. We wanted models and, the models wanted exposure.

Now, we had a camera and models. But, we did not have swimsuits. So, what we did was take a drive fifteen miles north to a neighboring college town. We spoke with several females about where they purchased their swimsuits. All roads pointed towards a small business in the city that sold swim suits and wet suits. After going in and speaking with the store manager for about fifteen minutes, explaining to him what we were trying to do and helping him to understand that by allowing us to use his swimsuits for a photo shoot we could help him generate business for the store within a market demographic that he was not yet exposed, he thought it was a great idea We put a contract document together to borrow some pieces, and two weeks later we were conducting our first photo shoot. We needed swimsuits and they needed free exposure.

The exposure was two-fold. The workers in the store were college students of the local university. They were not African-American, but they had dreams of becoming models as well. This gave us access to a market demographic that we had no idea that we would be able to penetrate. Not only did we network for photo shoot wardrobes, but our model base had almost quadrupled.

As we completed levels of the project, each of the next levels became more and more challenging. Now it was time to produce the sample. What we found out was that it costs considerably more to produce a sample than it did to create in bulk.

However, you must first create a sample, to determine what changes should be made to give your product the final desired appearance.

We found a local copy company in the adjacent city, who agreed to produce three samples for us at a slightly reduced cost. One week later we had our samples and, all of a sudden we were the talk of our school. TS Exposure was a swimsuit calendar company. Even females that refused to work with us initially were awed at our production. The models that worked with us were amazed at how they turned out to look in print form. It was crazy! A couple of my business school professors began to give me a lot of insight on things to do and to lookout for in regards to conducting business and business ideas.

With the sample calendar completed, we were able to begin having some serious conversations with established business people in the community. We shopped the calendar to local banks and small businesses to sponsor ads in the calendar. For a small fee, we placed ads in the calendars. The models received more exposure. The swimsuit store received exposure and our sponsors received exposure.

Everyone involved received something. Thus, as you create your business, determine who you can help and how as you help yourself. The same people and businesses that you need will in turn need you.

It was this business experience that made me realize that I really wanted to be a business person more than an architect. I was too deep into my major at that time to start over. However, changing to Construction Management, would allow me to keep my Architectural base, but to take more business classes. Then, once I graduated I would be able to get an MBA without the hassle of trying to complete a lot of undergraduate business courses.

You can talk about your Dreams forever. But, until you build your sample, you are just a Drcamer and not a doer. As we used to say, "Don't talk about it, be about it." If it is worth your time thinking about it, figure out how to do it. If it doesn't work, so what! At least you tried. That is more than what those who are laughing at you have done. Trust me, as soon as you create your sample, your doubters will become potential investors. Better yet, they will become your potential consumers.

There is no greater feeling than doing "the deal." I don't care what "the deal" is. My adrenaline really begins to pump when I am negotiating a business deal. If I am in a business deal, I am going to win. There is no way for me to lose. By any means necessary, everyone at the table needs to understand that my way is the best way and, there is no other way for them to think.

Call me, when you have your next "best idea you have ever had." And you will see.

CHAPTER 3

MARKETING & PROMOTIONS

Just as many other business ideas were stimulated by idle minds of college students trying to figure out ways to make money before they were cut off from their parents, so was one of my ideas.

My business partner and I had come to the conclusion that the only way out from having to compete in the corporate rat race as graduation approached was to own our own business. We had put our dibs in the swimsuit calendar thing. It was fun, but we had come to the conclusion that in order to really make it work, we would have to go national with it.

That is when the resources dried up on us. We didn't have the money to put behind the product going national. Understand that this was in 1993. We had no idea of an internet at that time. Selling a product on a regional or national level required major financial resources.

Rule #3: Know your Product

We created the product, we had the sample in hand, and, had actually sold copies. We began to researching mass manufacturing and production. We were evaluating our options. Should we go with a print shop, or a copy shop? Should we look at book distributors? How much would it would cost for us to go with either if we produced small quantities or, produce in bulk? How many units would we have to sell in order to break even? How many units will we have to give away as marketing, or consider to be loss or stolen? What would be our cost variance to manufacturing in the U.S., vs. oversees?

If your business concept is one producing any type of units, these are the mere basic questions you must answer in the business plan phase.

Where are you going to manufacture your units? Anything that can be produced anywhere else in the World, can be produced within the United States. The top issue with producing within the United States verses the producing in oversees (IE: India or China), is the cost to produce in the United States is often times higher. Higher production costs is going to mean either fewer units can be produced within the same budget or, the budget has to be increased to produce the same amount of units.

With the assistance of the world-wide-web, we are now able to communicate virtually in real time with manufacturing facilities around the World. Most facilities have someone on staff that are able to communicate in English which makes conducting international business relatively simple, just as speaking with someone in a neighboring state.

The reason why I rank marketing and production, one and two, is because without an actual product you have a Dream not a business. Without having the ability to market your product, you will end up with a box full of trinkets in your garage that you are not able to push.

Whenever, I am approached by a person that has just come up with their next "best idea they have ever had" I ask them two real quick questions to determine just how in depth I should go into the conversation. Question number 1: How are you going to produce the units? Question number 2: How are you going to market the units?

If you can answer these questions, you know your product and, you are ready to move on to the next phase. What is the next phase? Either you have answered these questions and realize that this is not a feasible mission. Or, you answer these questions and figure out the necessary steps to accomplish the project.

As we answered these questions, what we determined was that we did not have the adequate financial resources to continue the mission. So, in order to secure the resources we began to brainstorm ideas to raise money. To be quite honest we came up with some good ideas and some bad ideas, both legal and illegal. Our brainstorming ranged from calling home and asking Mamma for the money, borrowing the money from college friends to making investments into street pharmaceuticals. Yes selling weed. We were twenty-two year old college students, who believed in their idea. We were not going to let anyone, or anything, prohibit us from attaining our Dream. That included risking doing ten to twenty in federal prison.

However, we rethought that pretty quickly and, decided that we would throw some college parties instead. So we began promoting parties. Parties weren't the quick licks that we needed, but they were fun. We enjoyed what we were doing.

We were both very familiar with party promotion aspect. We had been in the same fraternity for the past couple of years and that was how we raised money as an organization. By being members of the fraternity, one the first Black Greek Letter Organizations, we already had a certain group of followers, who were willing to see that our parties were successful.

I had recently been elected as Student Government President and had access to certain local club owners and government officials who would give us a break on overhead expenses for facilities. Thus it was a matter of calling on the human resources that we had, as opposed to financial resources that we didn't have.

Even though we had human resources, we still had to do some grunt work. We had to inform those that were not a part of our immediate circle of who we were and what we were doing. This was our first real lesson in Marketing.

No matter whom you are or how great your idea is, if no one knows about your idea they cannot support it. You must determine who your target market is and how you can get the information to them. When I speak to people who have the "best idea they have ever had right now," this is one piece that I find they often overlook. They often believe that because their idea is so great, that someone will hear about it and all of a sudden it will go viral. Wrong!

Think about it. Before even the biggest business goes public, the notice of an IPO to be offered goes out months before the IPO is offered which is months before the business actually goes to public. Sometimes this may even be hyped or speculated a year or two in advanced. Financial gurus will tell you that this is for the protection of the potential stock holders. I say that this is the greatest marketing ploy of any publicly traded company. They hype up that the company is going to public. They speculate a dollar price per share. This gives notice to the World about this company, who some never would have even heard of, if an IPO was not being offered. This allows those who have never heard about the company, to now want to be a part of the "next best thing going on," to purchase shares of a company that isn't worth any more than the shares that are being purchased. However from the owner's perspective, he has created a global company since now 100,000 investors have invested $50 per share into his company. The IPO concept is marketing ingenuity!

You may be not be ready to create an IPO for your idea. However, you must have a solid marketing plan. How are you going to reach your target market? In the 60's we used radio. In the 70's we used local newspapers. In the 80's we used local TV. In the 90's we used banner ads on websites. In the 2000's we are using social media. All of these forms of marketing are still available and are great to use. However, you must determine which is best for you and your target market.

There is no better form of marketing than grassroots. This partners you with your idea that is shared by you in your World. Your World then spreads the word in their own little Worlds, which includes some that you are not affiliated. This form of marketing takes a little while longer to get the word out. However, this is a form marketing that gives you credibility as soon as it is distributed. General marketing requires those who are reached to perform a few extra steps to determine if your idea is credible. But, that grassroots campaign cannot have a value placed on it.

At the ground level, getting the word out about my products or services always started with my business cards.

However, business cards are typically an approach for business to business relationships and service oriented businesses relationships. When trying to develop a customer base for products that you are trying to establish a brand for, I like the more hyped approach of passing out fliers and hand bills.

Independent music artists have proven that this is a very successful approach. They tend to use wardrobes of shiny suits and blinged out jewelry to advertise their upcoming CD's.

Party promoters tend to use this approach as they advertise their next big event with fliers of sexy females wearing the type of attire they are promoting to be worn to the event. College party promoters go with the scantily clad bikini model look. After-Five party promoters go with the models wearing evening dresses displaying their hour glass figures.

I have actually done both. However, my most memorable flier was that for Kamaté Most Wanted (Figure 3.1). The mystique of this design grabbed the attention of our target market and, left those who did not know what Kamaté was, asking questions.

We used a concept for our fraternity parties that we termed "Coming Soon." All we placed on the flier were the words "Coming Soon" and an image that the

Yard associated with our fraternity. Thus, everyone on the Yard new that it was our flier and that we were about to throw some type of big event. However, no-one knew what the event was or when it would be held. As soon as we put the time and date out on a later flier, tickets for the event would be nearly sold out within days.

This was the same concept that we used for "Wanted." The flier itself made observers ask, "What is wanted? They asked "Who is wanted? They asked, "Who is Kamaté? They asked, "What is Kamaté? These questions are what provided the initial buzz about Kamaté. Weeks later we unveiled our Kamaté clothing line in fashion shows in Dallas and Kansas City. Before the end of the year, we launch one of the first urban apparel clothing lines on the internet.

WANTED
$1,000 REWARD
KAMATE URBAN GEAR
IF YOU GOT GAME, YOU GOT A GAME FACE. IT'S YOUR ATTITUDE. IT SHOWS THAT YOU CAN'T BE FADED. WHEN WEARING YOUR GAME FACE YOU BREAK'EM ALL OFF A LIL' SOMTHIN' SOMTHIN', REAL PROPER LIKE. PUT YOUR GAME FACE ON AT MANHATTAN'S FRESHWEAR IN BANNISTER HALL.
WWW.KAMATE.COM

Figure 3.1

Years later I created another business called My Hip-Hop Department. By this time there were hundreds of mainstream urban apparel companies. The internet had taken business opportunities to whole new height, way beyond our early days of Kamaté. Many Rap and R&B artists had launched their own clothing lines. Only a few of the fashion designers had entered the fashion game with us years before, were even still a part of the game. A couple of designers who had really made a huge dent in the business had actually sold their companies to national and international companies.

Even though these guys had made a lot of money through their music, I had a lot that I could offer them with my business knowledge. Thus, I created a website for My Hip Hop Department and began brokering individual deals with the clothing lines.

When urban apparel made its first big introduction to mainstream buyers, urban apparel stores were opening in malls all across the country. These were the only stores that were selling such items. Once major department stores, figured out that urban apparel was here to stay, they began to broker retail details with the designers and began selling the items at prices in which most urban apparel stores could not compete.

However rather than opening a store, I opened an urban apparel department store web-site. There, I carried nearly one hundred different urban designers, both mainstream and underground. Mainstream designers, were excited to have a new outlet to sell their gear and new designers were just as excited to have somewhere to sell theirs.

Creating the website was not nearly as expensive as opening a box in the mall to sell gear and it opened me up to a world of buyers rather than just a local retail base. By carrying some mainstream lines, credibility was given to the site as a reputable source for purchasing good quality clothing. Thus, those were loyal to certain brands made consistent visits to the site and consistent purchases on the site.

In order to really build up the buzz, I began to sponsor local events in the name of My Hip Hop Department.

One event that we sponsored was a college step show that was to be held during the weekend of one the major football games in the city. The step show was cancelled for whatever reasons shows and concerts are cancelled, but with our logo on the flier email lists that went out, our site's unique visitors went from about 8,000 per week to about 100,000 per week within the short period of time that the show was being promoted.

Though this was a grassroots appeal, we had struck a deal with a major model to host the event and to allow us to use her image on the flier. Needless to say this was a big hit. To this day, I still say if that event were to have taken place, we would have been on the verge changing the dynamics of providing space for urban apparel.

Another major contributor of grassroots marketing is advertising in local establishments, primarily restaurants where a large amount of your potential clients may visit. It is a good idea to attempt to create a partnership plan with a local establishment that serves as a win / win for both your business and the establishment.

Figure 3.2 shows a proposal presented to a local establishment. Outlined in the proposal is exactly what would benefit both parties entering such an agreement.

Figure 3.2a

Figure 3.2b

What's the Catch ?
BLUE CHIP GAMER
• Your waitresses and bar-tenders provide Blue Chip Gamer coasters when serving drinks.
• BlueChipGamer.com link banner is displayed on your website's homepage.
• Your waitresses wear double branded t-shirts on Saturdays.
• A frame 8 ½" x 11" poster is displayed at your front counter.
• THAT'S IT !!!
This is a confidential document is for proposal purposes only

Figure 3.2c

So my friend, know your product. Know your target market. Know how you are going to reach that market. Know what it is going to cost you to reach your market. Determine if you have some human resources available to you that will allow you to cut some costs. Whatever you do, do not overlook the marketing plan!

In undergraduate and graduate business class, I was always taught that there are Four P's of Marketing. The first P is "Product." Whether your business is selling widgets or selling a service, either your widget or your service is your product.

How you present your product, is going to determine how it is received by potential customers. If you understand that every product is a desire of someone and not a need, you are more apt to making intelligent business decisions. You may say, "My customers are hungry, and they are going to buy my hamburgers because they are the best around!" Correction my dear friend, if your customer is hungry, she is going to make the best decision due to her at the time. If she has very little money, her decision may be to go to a cheaper burger joint. If she has an excess of money, she may decide that she wants a sirloin steak rather than a hamburger. As a business owner, your marketing plan she as if no matter how much or how little a person can afford to spend, they are going to go the extra mile to purchase your product.

I was having lunch with friends not long ago. One friend is an Attorney and the other is a Real Estate Agent. Both of these guys provide services as their products, but they view their products very differently. The Attorney views her product in the form of billable hours. The Real Estate Agent views her product in contract values sold. Regardless of how they viewed their products, it didn't matter. What I wanted them to realize was just as a grocery store sells meat and a gas station sells gas, every business is in the business of selling a product to make a profit.

The second "P" in marketing is price. The Attorney sells her product (billable hours) at a rate of $150 per hour with a half hour minimum. The Real Estate Agent sells her product (contract value) at a rate of 7% of the value of the contract value. The grocery store sells beef at a rate of $1.50 per pound and the gas station sells gas a rate of $4.10 per gallon.

You get it? Every business has a product. Every product has a price. Whatever your product is, you must determine what your price is to sell it. The first thing you must do is determine the market rate. Are you looking to start selling your own magazine? OK, find seven other magazines similar to the one that you want to start and find the going price for those magazines. Hummm.... I bet they are somewhere in between $4.00 and $7.50 per magazine but if you buy an annual subscription, the rate would probably be 60% off the cover price.

So what does that tell you? If your magazine's price is outside the bell curve to the left of $4.00 or to the right of $7.50, your magazine's price is going to be questioned by your potential market rather quickly. The problem with new business is getting started. Since you are just starting your business and you are facing such a great deal of overhead, you tend to want to charge a little bit more to make up for some of the cost that you are incurring. I will warn you that is not the right approach to take. I understand you are producing widgets. Because you are not able to produce in bulk, your cost is more. Because your cost is more, you are not able to realize that 70% return on each widget as is customary in your industry. Oh you are a new Real Estate Agent and, you have to share your fee with your broker. So, since the law says that you can charge your client a maximum of 7% of but other local agents are charging 5%, you are keeping your rate beyond the bell curve because you need to make up that cost that you have to share with your broker.

My friend I must tell you that no matter what your product is, keep your price point within the bell curve until you get yourself and your reputation established. Once you have established yourself in the industry and gained a reputation for yourself, your clients and / or consumers will pay whatever your price you ask of them. But, don't try to make up for the money you have spent. Your business should be treated as a marathon and not a sprint. Plan your pricing around succeeding in the long run and not, trying to make all of your money back right now. Success will come. Don't price yourself out of business.

The third "P" is "Place." Place is simply where are you going to sell your product. If your product is a widget to be sold in a retail store, place will also include what shelf or where in the isle it will be displayed.

Now if you are selling widgets, most of the same rules apply that are used in selling services, with the addition of placing your product in a big box retail location. Big box locations are a little tricky. They all want to sell the latest and "hottest" items (products). It is up to you to convince them to carry your line of T-shirts or bar-b-que sauce in their stores.

Getting your product in the stores, may be the easy part. Getting your product maximum visibility is a another story. When you go to your favorite grocery store to buy your favorite box of cereal, you most likely go down the same isle you always do and select your favorite box of cereal off of the same shelf as you always do. This is known in the marketing World as product placement. In many cases the cereal producer may have a friendly handshake in place to see that their cereal is placed on the top shelf. The top shelf may be five feet and five inches from the ground. This is close to the average height of a female (those who do most of the shopping). If she looks straight forward from a standing position, she will be looking directly at the top shelf. At a maximum stretch of her arms, she should be able to reach to the point to where she can grab any product on the store at the middle of the box and safely secure it. This strategy is applied for approximately 90% of retail product placement.

If this same female decided that she did not want the product on the top shelf, she could slightly lower her eyes and find product on the next shelf. This product's supplier may not have had a handshake as intense as the top shelf product. But, it was firm enough to make the big box want to give the product good visibility to potential consumers.

At the very bottom, we find products that have suppliers fighting to gain maximum visibility, yet very excited to have its product even placed in the big box. If you are lucky and you create a good proposal, this is likely where you will end up initially (in the big box but at the bottom of the shelf).

I don't drink alcohol but, I have friends that do. Thus I have been in liquor stores and clubs. Product placement is why we use the term "top shelf." Top Shelf liquor is supposedly the best the club has to offer. You don't see it in a box on the floor. The bartender does not pull it from under the counter to pour it. When you ask for "top shelf," they turn and look to the top shelf and pull down its best. That's where you want your product, on the top shelf.

Becoming top shelf does not come fast and it is not easy. When your product becomes the desire of a vast majority of the consumers you are catering to, you will be on your way to Top Shelf! You can then start adding to your cost for those who want your product.

Place as it concerns to the service industry, is simply what physical location are you going to provide your service that will be most conducive to your clientele.

For example, if you are a barber or a stylist you may want to open near a shopping center or a mall to drive walk-in traffic. If you are Real Estate Agent, you may want to work out of your own home because, your showings will be at the homes of those that are trying to sell and your meetings will most likely be in your car or in the homes of those trying to sell or buy. If you are a general physician you may want to open up near a hospital, just in case you need to have your patients go immediately to the hospital. If you are an attorney you may want to office very close to the courthouse so that you will not have to leave your office an hour early to get to court on time. After all, time is money.

The fourth "P" (Promotion), is a hybrid of Price and Place. If you are in a service industry (IE: Attorney, Doctor, Real Estate Agent, Barber, Stylist, Financial Planner and etc...) your advertisement is your sales agent. You don't have anyone directing readers and viewers to your company. Thus you want your ad placed in the best possible location to attract the most viewers. Whether it is in a local newspaper, an internet website or a local magazine, the placement of your advertisement is crucial to attracting the attention of viewers. If you are advertising on local radio or television, the time slot in which your ad is running is just as crucial.

Running banner ads on websites is a great idea. But again, the placement of the banner ads can make or break you. Banner ads are sold in different sizes and show in different locations. A banner ad at the top of web page typically has more viewers and higher click-thru ratios than banner ads on the side of the page. Banner ads on home pages have a higher number of viewers than banner ads on sub pages. However, depending on the website you may have more potential customers who view certain sub pages than the overall customers who visit the homepage. Thus you may want your ad placed on the subpages in addition to, or in lieu of, the homepage.

I am a very big fan of internet marketing. When I create marketing plans for my clients, fifty percent of the plan includes internet. When we advertise on a radio stations, we hit their streaming listeners as well. When we advertise in community newspapers, we advertise on their website as well. The purpose for this many of those who listen to a radio station or purchase a community newspaper also visit the websites. However, all of those who are streaming or looking at the online versions, are already online and a click away from a purchase.

With that said, to say that every business should have a website is an understatement! If you have a license to do business, paid business taxes and etc..., your business is incomplete if it does not have a website. Get one!

Social Media Marketing is another form of marketing that you should like to develop into your marketing strategy. However, social media should be used very carefully. It is exactly what the name implies (Social). Many of those who will "follow" you or "friend" you will do so because they want to know what your business is doing.

Advertising to your Friends and Followers should be done so gracefully.

Don't attempt to send out coupons everyday to your Friends and Followers. Better yet, do so periodically. When you do post coupons, be sure to let them know that "Only your Friends and Followers" are receiving them or, at least are the first to know. This makes them feel special. Overloading their emails and social posts with coupons and advertisements, will be the fastest way to become an ex-friend.

To build your Followers and Friends, you should make subtle comments at least three to five times daily. Your Friends and Followers want to know that you are actually a person and not a machine with automated responses. Pick a different Friend or Follower and directly comment to everyday. You will be amazed at how many new Friends and Followers you will gain by doing this. They will be Friends and Followers to those you have commented to and, will begin to Friend and Follow you.

Again, this is Social Media Marketing. Do you think movie stars and professional athletes are commenting back to random fans and allowing them to Friend and Follow them because they are just super nice guys? Heck no! It is promotions. They allow you to Friend and Follow them. You get to hear comments they make before the media does (or at the same time). You then buy magazines in which they appear. You watch television shows in which they appear. You buy movie tickets in which they appear. You buy the jerseys in which they wear. Why? You do so because they are your "Friends" not just movie stars and professional athletes. They are your "Friends." If you didn't know it, your "Friends" are getting paid to have "Friends." Yes having "Friends and Followers" is big business. However, it is done so very discretely. Thus you too, must develop "Friends" and "Followers." But, you must treat them as "Friends," not potential clientele or customers. Otherwise your friendship will get dropped like a sack of wet bricks.

As social media evolves, so should your social media marketing campaigns. At the height of the dot com bubble, the number one social media marketing tool was the email e-newsletter. Every one with a website was using this form of marketing to reach their potential market, with hopes of others forwarding the newsletters on-line. This is still a much used vehicle to get information out; however the popularity of it has greatly decreased.

As the e-newsletter's popularity has decreased, there has become an increased in the use of Apps (mobile web applications). Apps are available on most smart devices.

With the proper development of an app, you will be able to promote your business with mobile web interaction. Understand that it is not enough for you to simply have an app; it must be entertaining for the end-user. It must be able to disburse information all while limiting the amount of time the end user must interact with it.

For instance, I often use an app that gives me a great deal of information about sports and sports score. The app also allows me to listen to live sports broadcasts, read quick news articles and play fantasy sports.

As a sports fanatic this is great. I have one source of information for all of my sports desires. As a business owner this is a great marketing ploy. The company is keeping all of my attention centered on receiving information from their company.

Thus this is how you should design your mobile app marketing project. Let's say you are a dentist. However, your app should not be boring and only have an appeal to other medical professionals. Your app should be sexy and one which allows patients and potential patients to enjoy a positive interactive experience. Your app should give a virtual tour of your office. No one wants to read a bunch of print on a six inch mobile phone screen. They want to hear a verbal presentation of the services that you provide. They want to click one button and be able to make an appointment. You know your chosen field of business. Now, you have to make it fun for your customers.

Create your app, make it fun and enjoyable for your users, your patients and your clients. If they like your app, they will join your other social media venues. This will give you an opportunity to gain visibility with them many times throughout a given month. The more visibility you have with one potential client, customer or patient the more visibility you will have throughout the network of their world.

CHAPTER 4

THE GREAT KAMATÉ

In most instances, you will have a good idea that will lead to an even better idea. Some people say this is being inconsistent. I call it simply the art of reinventing yourself. This is what we were faced with as we were developing our swimsuit calendar.

After-all we were researching types of swimsuits we wanted to use for our next calendar. We had caught the attention of several models who wanted to wear our gear. Several photographers had sought us out to work with us for the next shoot.

As we researched the swimsuits, the styles and the material, we began to ask ourselves a common question. If the suit costs $X retail, how much does it cost to produce? The answers we began to find were bananas! The average swimsuit selling for $75 - $125 had manufacturing cost of merely $4 - $8. It was crazy! But, it was clear. We were moving towards the wrong line of business. It was time we took our partnership to the next level. It was time to move into the fashion industry as we came up with concepts of our female swimsuit line.

Moving into this industry was not very easy, however, because it was fun and was something we loved to do, the challenges that presented themselves were what we considered to be low hurdles. Because of our past business experiences, we applied the things learned and used them as stepping stones for our next best greatest idea we ever had.

Unfortunately the time had come for us to graduate college and, we still had not created a company that would afford us the financial freedom of being young and rich before we received our college degrees. At that time, that was the day saddest day of my life. But, we were able get good jobs that would allow us to finance our capers and become productive citizens. So, I guess there was something positive that came out of this.

I enjoy working, but I enjoy working for myself even more. The way I had to look at it was my job was the bank for my company. We were requesting loans and lines of credit from major financial institutions to finance a project that most lenders questioned. How could a kid from Pine Bluff, AR with a partner from Jackson, AL become international swimsuit designers?

Our motto, just as many of the mid-twenty something's of Generation – X had become "Get rich or die trying!" And, designing female swimsuits was how we were going to get rich. Financing the project would be done through corporate paychecks.

Many of our friends had graduated with us. They were who we were pitching our ides to, so that they could invest into our business. Though at the time, we had no idea of what an IPO was, we had created one, and we were looking for investors.

If you are not having fun doing what you do, odds are you will not do it for long. Thus, when you create your business just Be You. I mean, BRAND yourself (your business) well! Your product or service is your brand. You must sell your brand just as you are attempting to sell your product or service.

Your brand is going to be the first impression of which a potential customer will take notice. You say you are an attorney. But, how do I know? Oh, this is your business card?

Your business card could be handed from one person to the next. The second and third persons to receive it may not be able to associate your professional personality with your business card. Thus, if your business card is made out of flimsy paper that could be taken as a reflection of the service that you provide. However if you have a nice linen card stock business card, your business may be reflected as very professional and one to be taken into consideration when soliciting legal services.

The attorney with the flimsy business card may be just as good as the attorney with the nice linen business card and maybe even better. The person with the best initial impression is going to receive the first call.

Some may say that this is not a fair way to assess whether a business is the most desired, simply because it has the nicest business card. I say that it is. You must take pride in your brand if you want your potential customers to respect your brand.

Probably the most important part of your brand is your logo. Your logo should be simple and used on every piece of literature and marketing material published by your business. Your logo can be an image. It can be a word. It can be initials. Regardless of what it is, it should be simple and used on every piece of literature and marketing material published by your business. This includes business cards, web-sites, letter head, company shirts, company caps and etc... If you give away promotional materials such as mouse pads, pens, pencils and etc... your logo should be on those items as well.

You want your logo to represent your business when you are not able to represent it yourself. When, I am traveling on the highway and I want a burger or need to get gas I look for the logos on the highway signs. When I see the logos with which I am familiar, I pull off at the designated exits. In essence, your logo is your business and, your business is your logo.

Create a logo that means something to you. Your world will consistently ask you what it means. The design of your logo should remain consistent. You should always use the "exact same" font and colors for the images and graphics for your logos. Images should be spaced exactly the same distance apart when using your logo.

When designing your logo, it is probably best that you work with a good artist or graphics designer. You want to work with someone that can capture your imagination and bring your logo to life. Your designer should be able to come back and provide you with an actual logo that is better than what you originally envisioned. If your designer needs to provide you with more than three samples for you to choose from, you are probably dealing with the wrong designer and should immediately select someone-else with whom to work.

The designer that I selected to create my first logo for Kamaté was a young man making copies of his drawings at the local copy store. I liked his drawings so much that I solicited his help in creating my logo. After sitting down with him for half an hour, giving him my business idea and logo concept he created a logo that my business partner and I later called Edō (Figure 4.1). Edō was the face of a man with dreadlocks, with eyes but no eyeballs. This was a concept driven by the idea that we could do anything we wanted and, that we had faith that we would be successful even without seeing.

We created a label that we placed on the inside of our clothing. The label itself was a logo design. Because the details of Edō were not good for such a small space, we just used a simple label design logo that we felt sent a very powerful message. We used the simple Kamaté text, the names of my partner and mine, the Roman numerals MCLXXI for the year 1971 which was the year we both were born, our tag line PUTCHA' GAME FACE ON!!!, attached with the numbers 11:1 to the logo. 11:1 symbolized the Bible verse of Hebrews 11:1, simply "Faith is the substance of things hoped for and the evidence of things not seen. See (Figure 4.2).

We also used a script version of the name Kamaté. This script, we normally displayed Edō. This was done so that when our customer base had decided that they were tired of wearing the large game face on their gear, that we would tone it down and use another logo that would already be associated with our business.

Figure 4.1

Figure 4.2

Kamaté emerged from our knowledge of female swimsuit price points while developing TS-Exposure. Our goal was to create a line of female swimsuits with the price points to be set between $50 and $200.

I created a few swimsuit sketches (See Figure 4.3 – 4.6) and sent them to my business partner and we kicked around many ideas centering the concept.

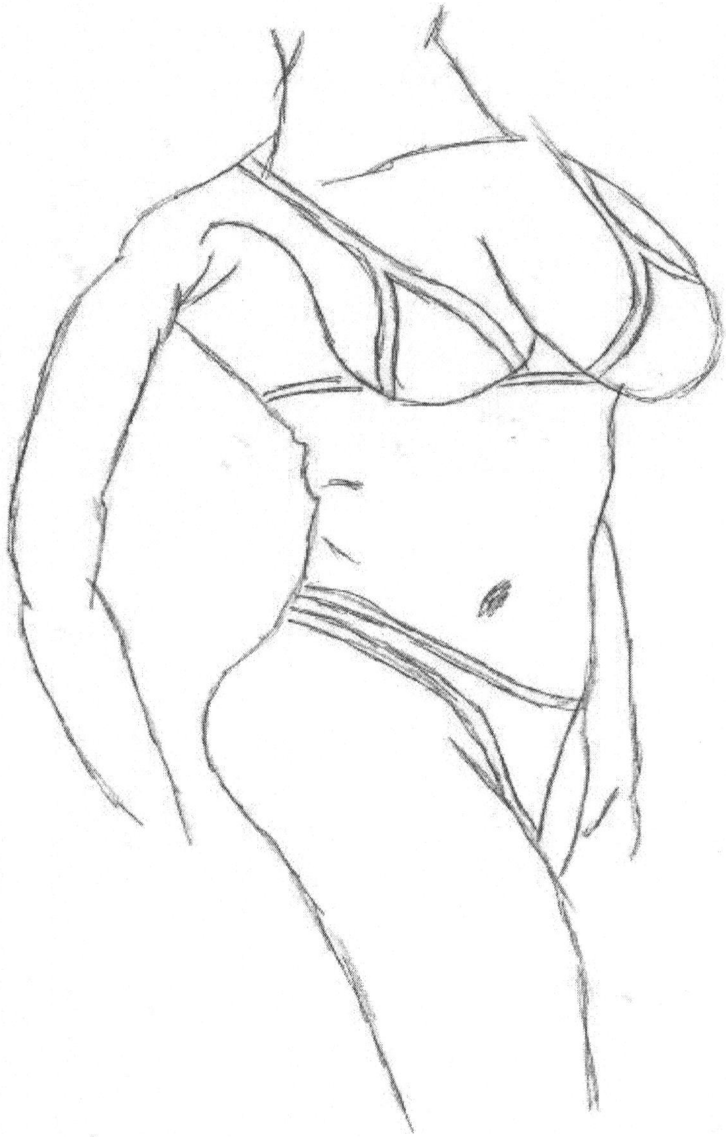

Figure 4.3

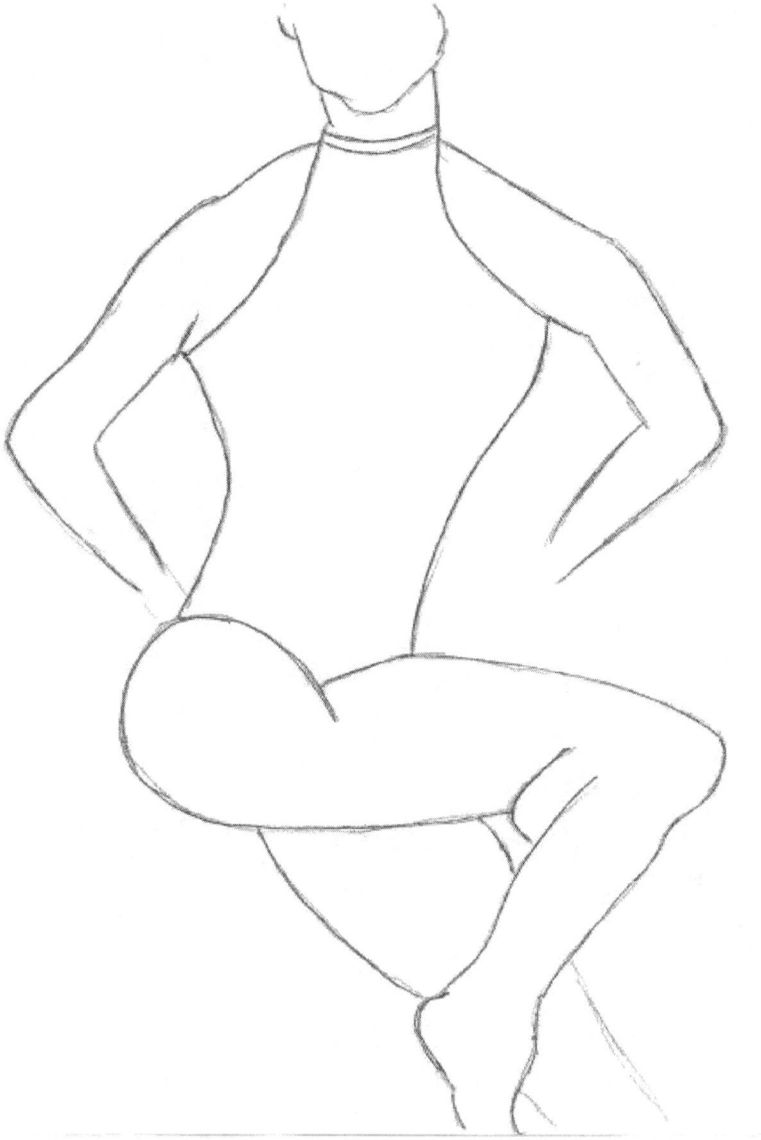

Figure 4.4

Figure 4.5

Figure 4.6

I located a seamstress near downtown Kansas City and took my design ideas to her. She suggested that I go to the local fabric store and select a pattern from which she could use as a base pattern to sew our sample pieces.

However, as we were in research mode, a very popular movement was taking place within the Hip Hop Culture. There were several fashion designers entering into the arena of hip hop fashions. Everywhere we looked new designers were introducing lines of baseball caps and T-shirts.

Rap videos had once been the feature of free advertisement for mainstream fashion designers. Those fashion designers had taken for granted that hip hop artists would wear their apparel for the simple fact that they were all they had.

However, young entrepreneurs that were involved in the hip hop movement but, were not actual singers or rappers started placing their own logos on caps and t-shirts and started draping artists in their gear. Those within the hip hop culture overwhelmingly responded and, began to support this new wave of designers.

Thus rather than continuing to solely focus on female swimsuits, we modified our business model and turned our attention to those we more closely identified, our hip hop family. I began creating sketches of hip hop gear and sending them to my business partner for his feedback. See Figure 4.7.

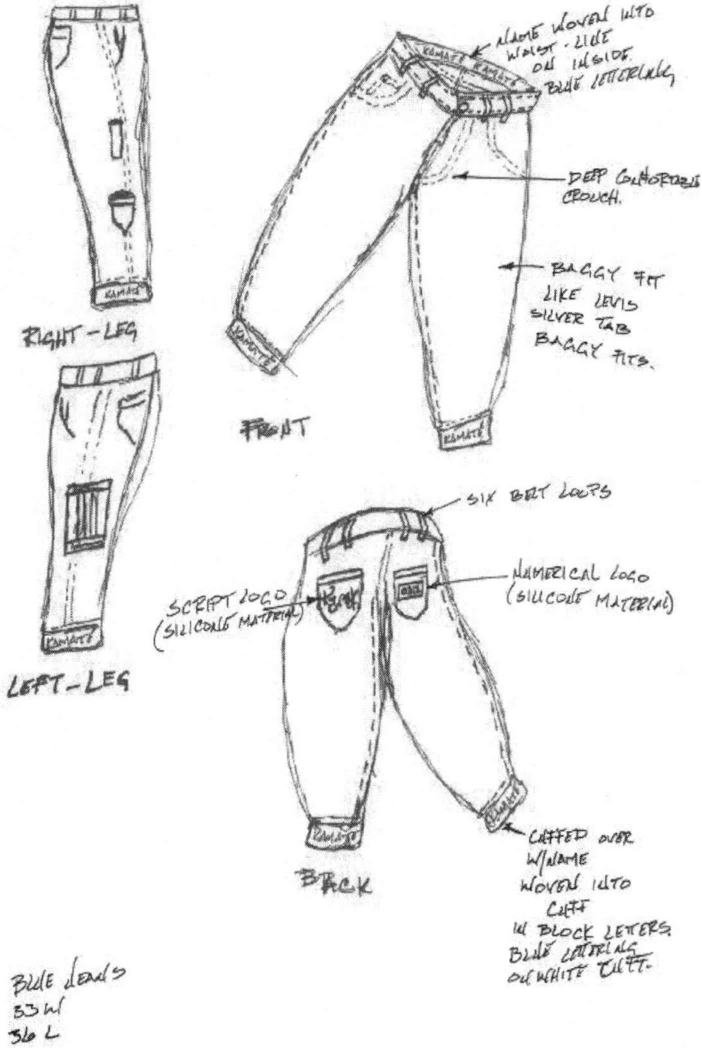
NAME WOVEN INTO WAIST-LINE ON INSIDE BLUE LETTERING
DEEP COMFORTABLE CROUCH.
BAGGY FIT LIKE LEVIS SILVER TAB BAGGY FITS.
RIGHT-LEG
LEFT-LEG
FRONT
SIX BELT LOOPS
NUMERICAL LOGO (SILICONE MATERIAL)
SCRIPT LOGO (SILICONE MATERIAL)
CUFFED OVER W/NAME WOVEN INTO CUFF IN BLOCK LETTERS. BLUE LETTERING ON WHITE CUFF.
BACK
BLUE JEANS
33 W
36 L

Figure 4.7

After a lot of research, we finally agreed and confirmed that Kamaté would become the name of our line of hip hop fashions. As we spoke to buyers of department stores, we quickly understood that "hip hop" was taboo when it came to trying to get lines placed in stores. Corporate buyers were using the term "urban." Whether this was good or bad, we had never figured out. However we began to use "urban" as well, so that we did not receive a stigma placed on our designs that was not accepted by major buyers.

We adopted the official name for Kamaté as Kamaté Urban Wear. It would become a line of urban apparel that was marketed to those who were considered to be a part of the Hip Hop Culture. We had already created a sample piece with our new seamstress. The original design is displayed in Figure 4.8.

We already had models that were signed to our line, so as we made the easy transition from female swimwear to urban apparel we began to showcase our line with our one sample piece in local fashion shows. See Figure 4.9.

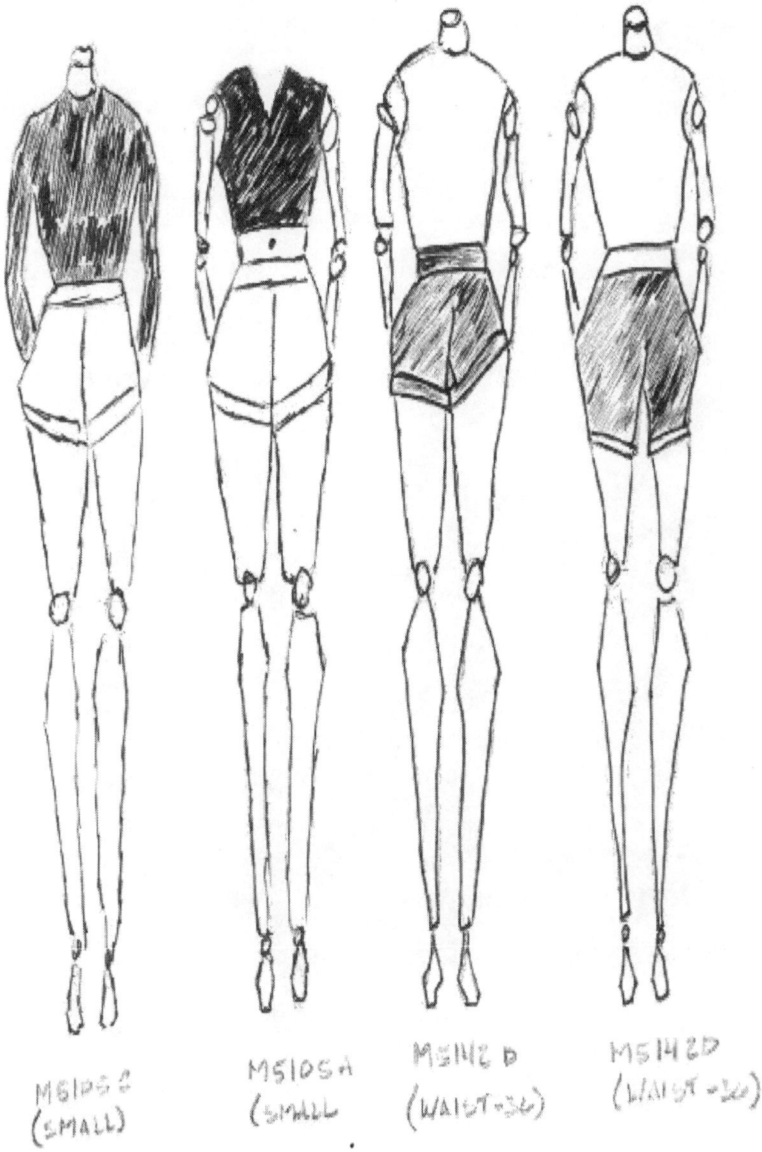

Figure 4.8

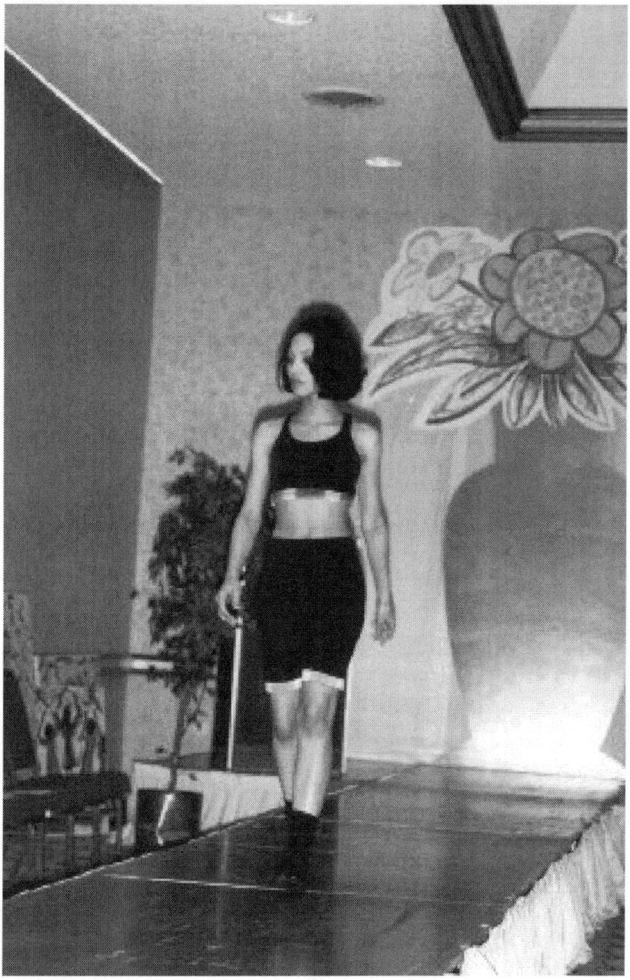

Figure 4.9

We began increasing our knowledge of

the fashion business. We began building our manufacturing capabilities through some very strategic business to business alliances. While doing so, we were quickly increasing our product line. From female swimsuits, our line evolved into baseball caps, t-shirts, letterman jackets, sweatshirts and more.

We began targeting as many aspiring rappers, R&B singers, models, actresses, comedians and DJ's as possible to place Kamaté on their backs. Our street credibility rating began to sore! Approval and acceptance from groups of our peers was growing by leaps and bounds as well. We were spotlighted on local radio stations, newspapers and in local magazines. Our gear was seen in national hip-hop videos and worn by very prominent rap artists.

Figure 4.10 shows a newsletter that we

Volume 1, Issue 1 January 19, 2000

Kamaté Newsletter

972 - 699 - 1191 www.kamate.com 816 - 761 - 4019

Blu-House Models For Kamaté

Magic International:
Booth 62125 - Sands Convention Center

Kamaté continues to gain momentum within the rap community. After first appearing on "Dranked Out", the initial album released by Blu House Recordings featuring the 903 Playas, Kamaté has recently extended its endorsement contract with Blu House to include new label artist D. Elli$. Check out music samples on Kamaté TV at kamate.com.

Figure 4.10

produced to spread the word about what was going on with the line and who were the latest endorsers.

If you are serious about creating your own fashion line, there is one major apparel trade show that you must attend in Las Vegas. Every major retailer attends this show to determine the latest fashion trends.

In order to fully show your line, you must rent booth space and create your space to be as much like a store with a corporate feel as possible. I must warn you that to really do your line justice you will have to invest a great deal into it. You must also market to the buyers, letting them know that you will be at the show and attempt to schedule as many on-site meetings at your booth as possible.

Figure 4.11 is a flyer that we used to attract buyers to our booth. The design of the flyer gave the feel of local hip hop magazines. This assured the buyers that we were in fact in touch with our target market. It also, gave the buyers assurance that we were not just hoping that having our product placed in their stores that we would consider that to be marketing enough. We were showing them, that by placing our products in their stores that they would reap the benefits of our marketing as well.

THE KAMATÉ SPECIAL EDITION
DA' SOURCE
THE MAGAZINE OF HIP HOP, URBAN CULTURE AND POLITICS
MONIE
IN THE MIDDLE OF KAMATÉ
FROZTEA & PUGHROK
THE KINGPINS BEHIND KAMATÉ
D - ELLIS
SPITN' LYRICS WITH HIS GAMEFACE ON !!!
BLUE HOUSE
THE LABEL THAT CHRIS MADE
KAMATÉ URBAN WEAR
SPRING MAGIC SHOW 2000
LAS VEGAS, NV
FEBRUARY 14 - 17
THE SANDS CONVENTION CENTER
BOOTH #62125
IF YOU GOT GAME
YOU GOT A GAME FACE.
IT'S YOUR ATTITUDE !!!
FEBRUARY 2000 . NO. 312

Figure 4.11

THE NATIONAL NEWSPAPER
KAMATÉ
TODAY
Story on 2B
kamate.com
NO. 1 IN AMERICA . . . FIRST WITH READERS
The
Logo That
Says Something
PRODUCTS
KAMATÉ URBAN WEAR
Magic Show 2000
Booth 62125 Sands Conventional Center
Las Vegas, NV - KAMATÉ Urban Wear is to be
the feature attraction at Booth #62125
in the Sands Covention Center in
Las Vegas, NV during the 2000 Spring
Magic Show. KAMATÉ will be bringing
in several of its major endorsers to model
its gear at various times of the show.
The show will be held February 14 - 17
in Las Vegas, NV. This will be KAMATÉ's
first Magic Show Appearance.
The company is expecting rave revues from
retail buyers all around the country.
Urban Swimsuits for the Urban Girl
By KAMATÉ
Team KAMATÉ
KAMATÉ is taking the urban universe by
storm with its fleece winter gear and
denim made for year round.
Story on 3B
Stay warm & be cool
Denim
&
Fleece
By
KAMATÉ
Magic Show 2000, Sands Convention Center
Booth #62125

Figure 4.12

Figure 4.12 is a second flyer that we sent to buyers to promote our site at the trade show. This flyer was more of design of a major newspaper. It allowed us to demonstrate that we were willing to increase a brand recognition on a more global scale.

When you are attempting to have your line placed in retail stores, buyers want to know your marketing plan. Showing them what you are doing, beats trying to tell them. Even though questions still will come, you can eliminate some of the basic questioning and dive right into how your marketing plan is going to benefit their stores by selling your line.

We were also prepared for the possibility that not every meeting was going to produce a major deal right there on the spot. We knew that we needed to have a catalog that we could place in the hands of the buyers. This would allow them to go back and make some intelligent decisions as to how much of our product they needed to have placed in their stores.

Figure 4.13 shows a page of our catalog. We felt that it was very important to have a catalog with actual models to give the buyers a real feel of how our gear looked on real people.

Figure 4.14 shows our product line of just the products. By showing just the product we were able to demonstrate the wide range of products that we carried.

All caps come in (A) Red, (B)Black, and (C)Blue.
All caps come in Flex Fit or Snap Adjustable (except KC-107 & 109).

Figure 4.13

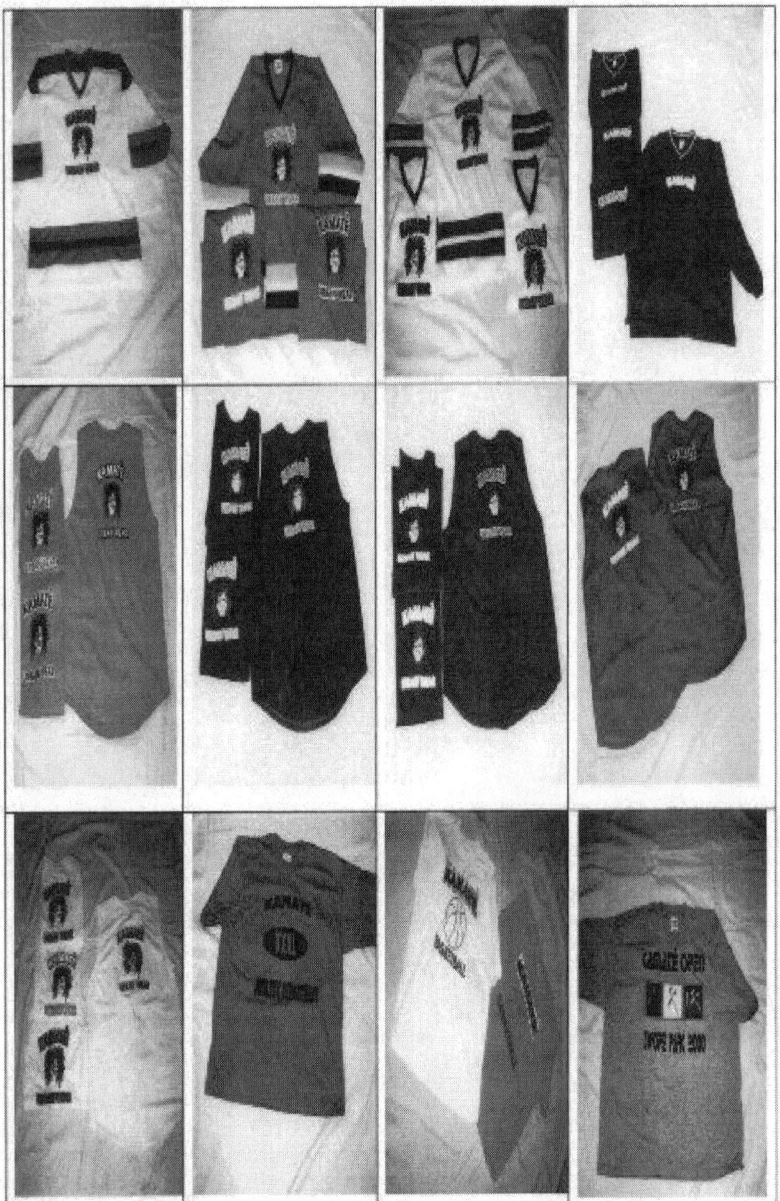

Figure 4.14

Every industry has a major expo or trade show in which the "big boys" participate. For the fashion industry, as with most industries, the show is held twice a year in Las Vegas. You should identify what show is affiliated with your industry and try to determine how you can get included.

Figure 4.15 displays images of our booth that we created for our major show. Most shows and expos take place three to four days. You can expect to spend $30,000 to $250,000 when you factor in all costs to participate. This includes food and lodging, booth rental, booth build-out, display products and marketing to your potential buyers.

Figure 4.15

It was the logo that was creating all of our hype and, we placed it on everything!

Every logo should have some type of meaning that is symbolic to your entrepreneurial venture, struggles or travels. If not, then it is only a picture that can be colored by a baby in coloring book with crayons.

CHAPTER 5

THE MAKING OF SASSY

Years after the concept of Kamaté, my dream of having a female swimsuit line still lived on. Nothing beats historical data. No one could rob me of my ideas. They were locked safely away in my mind. I knew what it would take to create the line. I knew the costs that I would be faced with in order to make it happen. So, I took everything that I learned during the research and development of Kamaté and, created Sassy Girl Fashions.

With this venture, I created my own logo for the fashion apparel. By this time, I had a pretty good amount of knowledge of about software that designers used. This logo was simply the word "Sassy," written in a specific font. Though the logo did not have a very deep meaning, it was symbolic. “Sassy” is a term for a female who has a very high self esteem. It is not a negative connotation. However, she has to be secure with herself to call herself “Sassy.”

In today’s World, a business is not official without a website. Many web template providers offer free website hosting. However, your business associates are able to identify whether or not you are playing business or really have a legitimate operation just by looking over your website.

There are some key links and pages, depending on your type of business that you must have on your website. Free websites are also filled with advertisements of many companies that support the free hosting.

Thus if you are serious about promoting your business, you should avoid the free versions of those websites and at a minimum purchase the basic hosting plan. These plans often times have templates that will allow you to begin creating your site and have some type of web presence.

As you develop your business, you should also develop your website. Just about every industry known to man also has a company that specializes in developing websites just for your type of business. A quick internet search will reveal these entities. These companies provide you templates and website hosting that looks more professional than a basic hosting package.

Another option is to purchase an actual web template of your specification and customize it to your liking. This does call for a certain degree of understanding of HTML, having the correct web development software and purchasing a hosting plan that will allow you to upload your site and site content to your hosting control panel. This is not too terribly difficult. This is actually the method that I prefer. It is very cost effective as well. Be sure you understand if your computer operating system supports the web development software you are researching before you make the purchase.

If you have the finances, you can actually solicit the work of a professional web developer to create your website. I have done this in the past. To be honest, unless you have someone that has the same interest that you have in mind, you will probably end up spending more time and money on a project that you are going to trash months after it has been completed.

I contracted with a freelance designer for a nominal fee to put the site together for me. The buttons at the top of the page give the descriptions of the different types of items that I had available for sell. There are additional links at the top of the page that allowed site visitors to contact my customer service department, create accounts, shop, and determine order status.

Depending on your type of business you should give your visitors and your customers a full range of communications just as if they were shopping in an actual location. Give them access to as much information as they may request, without having to speak directly with you. This will allow you to recognize your business making money while you sleep.

If you decide to take one of the initial options and create your own site, you can later hire a professional to add the finishes touches. This will allow you to have a much more desirable project at the end. Always keep in mind that no-one else can Dream your Dream. You will have to present your Dream to anyone you partner with to provide assistance.

Before contracting with someone to create your website, you should understand their full contract scope of the project. The designer that I contracted for this project only assumed the responsibility of graphic design. He did not assume the responsibility of coding in HTML. I only realized this once I had paid him the initial deposit.

He had a partner that he brought in to one of our meetings, that was to do the coding end of the project. However, at that point they made it clear that the design fee was not a part of the coding fee. The coding fee was approximately triple the amount of the design fee. Thus what I thought was a nominal fee to design a website, would in fact turn out to be an astronomical cost if I did not take control of the project.

Needless to say, we ended that agreement right at that moment. I did have the designs digitally for which I had already paid. I took those designs and, with my prior knowledge of mobile device programming I created and coded the site myself.

Had I really interviewed the guy the way I should have, this never would have become an issue. But, had I not had him sign a contract to release me the rights to the designs once the final payment was made, he could have held the designs hostage until I signed on with his partner to pay for the coding. In business, everyone is out to win. It is up to you to make sure you are not losing.

With the increasing speed of mobile technology, if you have a website, you should see that it has an easily convertible mobile version for mobile devices. More mobile devices are visiting web-sites every minute. Users of mobile devices are not trying to read internet pages, they are trying to access information as quickly as possible.

The look and feel of your mobile website should very closely resemble that of your full site. Your customers are looking for the links on your full site to be similar if not the same on your mobile site in order to quickly find the points of which they are searching from the mobile devices.

If you're business is one of selling widgets, your mobile visitors should be able to make purchases with ease. If your business is one of selling services, your site should make available to your customers the ability to schedule appointments.

While creating your full website and your mobile website you should also incorporate the design of your social media sites. More users are using their mobile devices to access social media sites than visiting specific websites. Thus, your social media pages should be as attractive as possible to ensure that your customers want to visit your social sites, follow you and friend you.

With the development of your web presence, you should also customize your social media sites. Most social media sites allow you to create some form of page profile customization.

In most instances, with just a few search terms with your specific social media pages, you can use key words to get customization instructions. A simple internet search will help you get instructions as well. I had the web guy to create a custom social media template for me, prior to our mutual separation. See Figure 5.1.

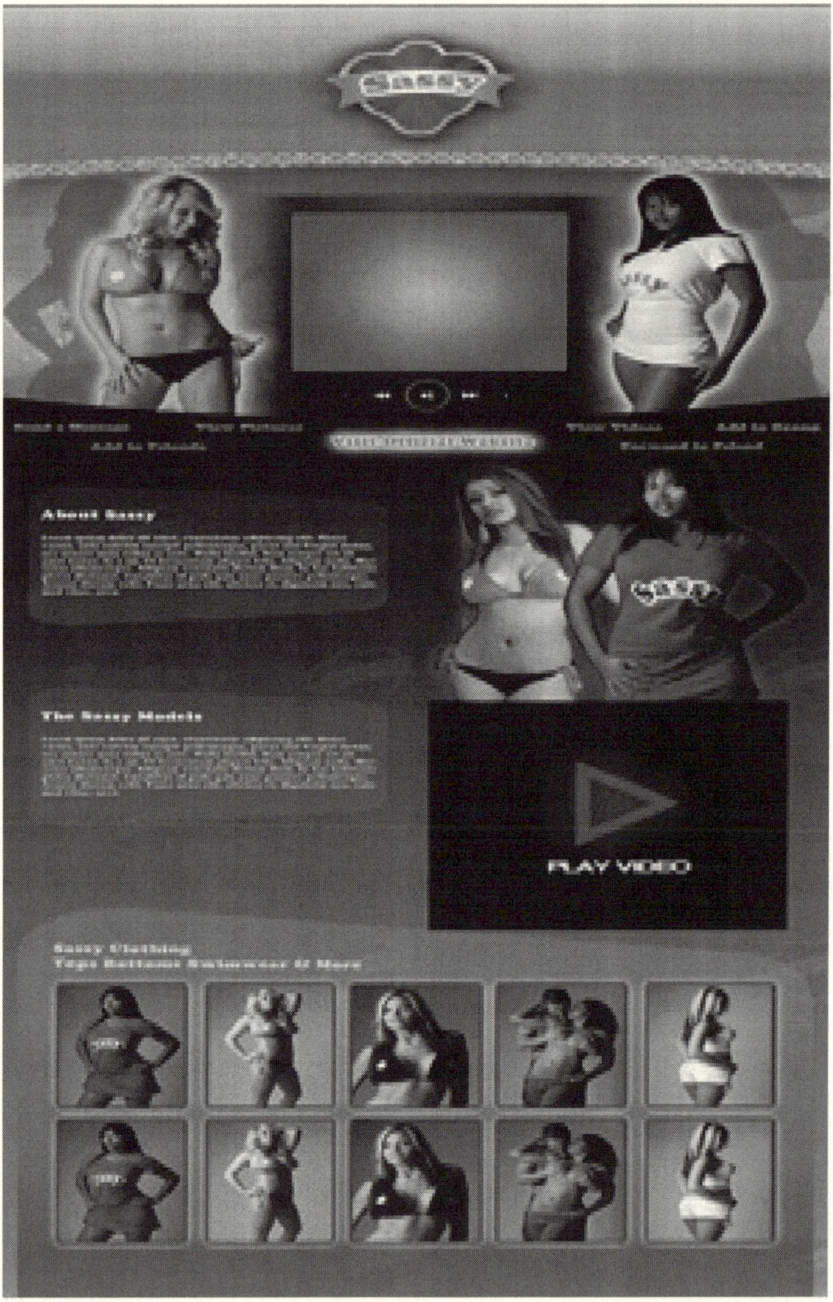

Figure 5.1

CHAPTER 6

ONE GREAT IDEA LEADS TO ANOTHER

Rule #4: Know your Costs for Doing Business

For most entrepreneurs starting their first or second venture, they tend to find that financing their ventures is typically the most challenging feat. Most times this is the death a Dream. Rather than researching financing opportunities, when a new entrepreneur reaches the "How much is this going to cost me phase?" they more often than not give up and just talk about the idea they used to have.

As soon as you come up with your *next best idea you ever had*, create a list of costs. These costs should include: Marketing Costs, to determine how much money you are going to spend to get your idea out to your target market. Depending on your idea, you may want to use print (local newspapers and magazines). The upside to using local newspaper is that you can develop a following within your community. The downside to using local newspaper is that the marketing range is very broad. Many of the readers may not be a part of your target market.

You may want to use local radio. Radio, hits a large volume of a segment within your target market rather quickly. The downside to using radio is that if you have a small budget, the number of listeners at a given time may miss your commercial. Advertising on the radio is paid for in what is called "spots." A spot is a time frame in which your advertisement is played on the radio station. Spots are normally purchased in thirty second increments. However, it is not unusual for spots to be purchased in fifteen or sixty second increments.

Today's technology is dictating the available and most effective means of marketing your products. Advertising on different websites is a good form of advertising. You can create banner ads that link to your website.

Most radio stations are streaming live. You can stream your radio commercial to online listeners rather, than advertising over traditional radio. This is a great forum for advertising if you have a website. The listeners are already online and, are a point and click away from going ovcr to your site as they listen online.

Questions you should ask your radio media salesperson include but should not be limited to: (1) What is the size of your listening audience? (2) How many times do you project a listener to hear the ad? (3) What are the demographics of your listeners? (4) What time spot do you project to be your hottest? (5) Who creates the advertisement, you or them? (6) When is the deadline to have all content turned in and ad paid for? (7) Do you offer online streaming advertisements? (8) Do you offer advertisement opportunities on your websites? (9) Do you offer adverting in weekly newsletters and email blitz campaigns? These are the mere basic questions that you will want to have answered.

Remember, these guys are in the business of radio. Most of the additional forms of marketing are extras for them. It does not hurt to ask how you can get those extra services for free. More often than not, those services may just require that you purchase so many radio spots. Ask!

Just about every potential target in your market has a cell phone. Most are using text messaging. Create a marketing plan that can develop your customer data base of text message numbers. There are many ways to create mass marketing via text messaging.

Community newspapers are another great source for advertising. Community newspapers are very much different from local newspapers. Community newspapers have a more direct reach approach as opposed to the broad reach of local newspapers. Community newspapers focus on particular segment of readers. The segment may be a specific neighborhood or suburb, a specific age group (Generation X or Y), a specific social behavior (party goers or politician) and etc...

Figure 6.1 is an advertisement that I ran in a community newspaper for a video game tournament that I promoted under my company name of Blue Chip Gamer.

BLUE CHIP
GAMER
presents
MADDEN 10
TOURNAMENT
$500 CASH PRIZE
Saturday, February 27th
Hilton Hotel • Allen, TX
For 24/7 Tournament Information
Text PLAY to 411247 or
www.BlueChipGamer.com

Figure 6.1

BLUE CHIP GAMER
presents
MADDEN 10
TOURNAMENT
$500 CASH PRIZE
Saturday, February 27th
Hilton Hotel • Allen, TX
For 24/7 Tournament Information
Text PLAY to 411247 or
www.BlueChipGamer.com

Figure 6.2

Figure 6.2 is an advertisement of the same tournament that I ran in the community newspaper for the video game tournament, that I promoted under my company name of Blue Chip Gamer with an African-Model.

This ad was run the following week and, demonstrated the diversity of the tournament. It is very important to show maximum inclusion when you are trying to include all within a product or service as your target market.

Very similar to community newspapers and local newspapers are national, local magazines and community magazines. National magazines are more specific to a target market group than newspapers.

They are able to hit a very large volume of your target on a national scale quickly and often. Advertising in a national magazine can be as specific targeting your audience, as a community-based newspaper. It is like advertising in communities just like yours all over the country. Often times a national magazine will advertise opportunities available for specific regions of the country. Thus, you will be able to advertise with a greater reach than locally but, with a much smaller reach than nationally. This can help reduce your budgetary concerns.

Advertising in local and community based magazines is very much similar to advertising in community newspapers as well.

Questions you should ask your print media salesperson include but should not be limited to: (1) What is your total circulation? (2) How often do you distribute copies? (3) How many times do you project an issue / copy to be viewed? (4) What are the demographics of your readers? (5) What issue do you project to be your hottest issue? (6) Who creates the advertisement you or them? (7) When is the deadline to have all content turned in and ad paid for? (8) Also ask about potentially advertising on their website. Many readers like to go online and read articles of their favorite local papers as well.

Figure 6.3 shows the same video game advertisement being advertised on the homepage of the community newspaper affiliated with Figure 6.1. Though some of the viewers are the same, many of the viewers are very specific to either the hard copy paper or, on-line site viewers. However, the demographics of the paper are pretty much the same. Thus, you should attempt to hit your target market in as many ways as possible.

BLUE CHIP
GAMER
www.bluechipgamer.com
MADDEN 10 TOURNAMENT
$500 CASH PRIZE
FEBRUARY 27TH | HILTON HOTEL | ALLEN, TX
For more information, text: PLAY to 411247

Figure 6.3

These are the mere basic questions that you will want to have answered. However you should dissect every inch of whatever print media you are pursuing to advertise in and jot down as many questions as possible.

Marketing is one of the most important, if not the most important expense for which needs to be accounted. The other expense that ranks either number one or number two with marketing is the production expense.

CHAPTER 7

GOING WIRELESS

In August of 2000 I was living in Kansas City, MO. A good friend of mine was working for a small company in St. Louis, MO. He told the owner of the company, that I may be a good fit to help steer the company in the direction in which he was envisioning. Thus I went to visit and interviewed with the company. The match seemed to be great. The only caveat was that my wife was still in school in Kansas City. Thus the arrangement that we worked out was, that I would live in St. Louis during the week and commute over the weekend.

Driving from St. Louis to Kansas City is approximately a three and a half hour trip one way. Most of the trip was through dead radio area. I was convinced that with as much technology as we had at the time that there had to be some way that I should be able to listen to the radio either over my cell phone or, over some handheld device. After-all the entire World had survived the greatest technology scare of all time, the Y2K internet crash! Looking back on that, now that was funny.

The majority of my friends were either mechanical or electrical engineers. They worked for some of the biggest engineering companies in the World. I began bouncing ideas off of them to see what they thought of the concept of being able to listen to any radio station in the country at any time.

Of course they were scientists and, their approaches to answering the questions were very scientific and theoretical. This was something that had not been done, thus how would I be able to develop such a product not having an electrical engineering or mechanical engineering background? This was the common question. My answer was, I didn't need the background if had competent and capable people who could give me the answers that I needed.

After, spending a few hours in the room with them, pitching this concept, at one of my college roommate's bachelor party, I actually received the best input ever. One the guys asked, "What are the Engineering Journals and magazines saying about this?" Another said, "I heard about a satellite radio that will be offering something similar."

At that point, I had enough to go on. I wasn't aware of engineering journals and magazines. However, it only made sense because; I always read the Architectural and Construction Management Journals. When, I got back to Kansas City I went straight to the bookstore. What did I find? several engineering magazines that were highlighting two new computer languages for coming wireless and mobile devices. The languages were Extensible Mark-up Language (XML) and Java 2 Mobile Edition (J2ME). I Wasn't a computer programmer. But I had plenty of friends from school who were. I was sure that I was going to be able to make a couple of phone calls and see which one had experience in writing code for the languages.

To my surprise, after speaking with my three prime resources after a period of several weeks, what I had learned was that the average computer programmer was not yet writing such code. Only one had even heard of it and, the others were like "Huh? You are trying to do what?"

It was at that point, that I realize that I was onto "the best idea I ever had." It was new. It was innovative and 99% of the World had no clue about it. However what I also realize was that if a little old country boy like myself from Arkansas could have dreams of creating such technology, there was someone else out there that may have been smarter or had more money to fund such a project and was doing so as well.

That is when I went back to discuss the project with my original business partner. We had gone through a borage of business ideas. If anyone knew how serious I was about trying to figure this new technology out it was him. After we sat down for several hours per day over the course of a weekend, the one thing that he said I knew I had to act on was this, "You have several aspects of the business that have to be completed. They include Research and Development, Product Development, Engineering, Marketing and Project Management." I agreed. My next question was what order do you think I should proceed in getting these phases completed and, how much time do you think I have before someone-else would be launching a similar project? His answer was simple. "All of the phases have to begin now and worked simultaneously and, you have about six to twelve months to get this project to market."

As I began to initialize the project phase I began to research what companies may have interest in partnering with me or even purchasing the concept from me. The first thing I did was start the planning of getting a patent on my idea.

Of course my initial concept was one that provided wireless communications to allow users to access radio stations and television stations from around the country using their mobile phones.

With the emerging of new technology, I also understood that radio and television media would not be the sole source of reasons why customers would want to purchase such devices. They would want to play games and view quick content such as the Page forty-three Beauty of the Weeks. This type of content, I called "sticky content." Sticky content is what I considered to be cheap, easy to create and would keep customers purchasing new content on a regular basis.

Sticky content, allowed me to create my own content, while I was attempting to work the deals to attain the rights to broadcast content of the major media providers. Thus, I began to work with local rappers to create music for content to be sold on my devices. I also began to work with local modeling agencies and photographers to build a portfolio of female swimsuit models to sell as screen savers and wallpaper on my mobile devices.

Figures 7.1, 7.2, 7.3 and 7.4 are images of swimsuit models that I used for the mobile screensavers and wall paper content.

Figure 7.1

Figure 7.2

Figure 7.3

Figure 7.4

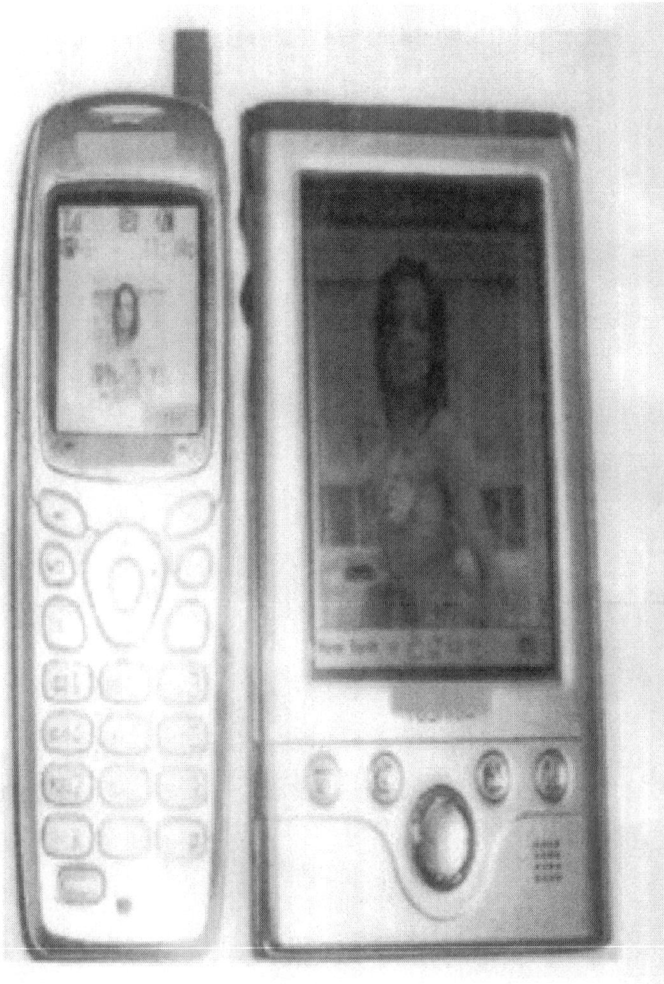

Figure 7.5

Figure 7.5 displays my mobile wall papers and screen savers on a mobile phone and a PDA. The images at the time were downloaded using wireless application protocol (WAP).

Today we are able to install our own images on our mobile devices. We are even able to create the images from our mobile devices, utilizing built-in cameras. At the time when I created WAR-B, mobile technology was not that far advanced.

Wireless phone carriers were in a race to 3G. They were in search of wireless app developers who they could strike deals with, in order to distribute their content to the mobile subscribers.

Thus at the time, images of female swimsuit models were something of which had never been heard. This was a phenom that could transcend mobile entertainment.

However, I had a choice to try to get mobile phone carriers to partner with me in order to have my wireless code placed in their mobile phones, or I could go out and create my own device using mobile technologies.

Going on my partner's advice, I did both. It was time to seek getting a patent.

The patent phase, I found was very paper work intensive. It was not too terribly difficult to understand. However the steps of getting a patent are very specific. If the documents are not completed exactly as requested, your patent application will be denied and you will probably lose your application fee (approximately $500).

When I was putting together my patent application, the primary question was what did my device look like? This was my "form factor." The device I was attempting to create had the similarities of a small cell phone. The material used to make it was to be of a stainless steel with a glass cover. At the same time, I was looking to patent the code that I had developed as well. The code was a mobile device computer programming code that I taught myself in the research phase of the project. I had created the code using J2ME to stream content from national radio stations over the wireless internet.

Of course, streaming multi-media content is not too terribly big in terms of today's technology. But this was in 2000 / 2001. The term "3G" or Third Generation Technology was just being introduced to industry professionals. The concept of listening to Hip Hop radio personalities on a radio station in New York City, while living in Kansas City and driving to Panama City seemed about as farfetched as Captain Kirk asking Scotty to beam him up in a Star Trek episode.

Regardless of how absurd others believe your idea to be, if it makes sense to you, follow thru. Either you will act on it now, or someone-else will act on it later.

Back then, there were several major wireless communication companies that I contacted to set up meetings with to discuss partnering. After several months of research, I quickly learned that there was really only one major player that was as cutting edge as the technology that I was attempting to introduce. This came about because of the technologies that were available at the time being used by the mobile communication carriers.

One technology that was being used at the time was TDMA (Time Division Multiple Access). This was simply how fragments of data were distributed over the wireless internet. Simply put when you speak on your mobilc phonc, your words are sent in packets distributed by increments of time.

Another technology that was being used was CDMA (Code Division Multiple Access). With this technology as you speak on your mobile phone your words are computed as data and packaged as packets of code and distributed to your listener. The packets may not be distributed in the sequence in which you say them. However, when they get to the other end prior to getting to your listener they are placed in the correct order and the listener on the other end hears what you have just said.

GSM and EDGE were other forms of technology that were being used at the time. They performed similarly to TDMA and CDMA; however they were being utilized primarily in European countries. The technologies were far more advanced than the options in the United States and were more capable of maintaining the systems that I was trying to develop. However, my resources did not allow me to attempt a global launch at that time.

With that in mind, as I created the code using J2ME, I had to make sure the wireless carriers would be able to integrate such code. My finding was the most popular wireless carrier at the time was playing around with J2ME as well. Wouldn't you know, the same carrier is the carrier that was headquartered not too far from the apartment complex in which I was living. After making several phone calls to the headquarters, I was put in contact with New Business Development. In turn New Business Development also put me in contact with Research & Development (R&D). With me being a potential minority vendor,

R&D put me in contact with the Diversity Department. The Diversity Department in turn put me in contact with Supply Chain Management. Supply Chain Management put me in contact with another potential vendor who had submitted a concept of compression software that would allow for feature length films to be streamed over a set-top box utilizing the technology of the mobile phone carrier. With my coding to stream multi-media and, the compression technique it would be only a matter of time before we would be able to create an entertainment media of the future.

This was all the beginning of some of the most intense meetings that I had ever participated in, and far greater than I could have ever imagined. I created presentations upon presentations for each of the various departments.

My concept put in layman terms was simple. I wanted to be able to listen to any radio station, or watch any television station that I wanted to over a wireless device.

When applying for a patent, the most specific of details is what sets your invention apart from other inventions that are similar to yours. There was no inventions released to the public, at that time, that were similar. That is not to say that there were no inventions in the making with projected release dates pending by other inventors. So, as I began working on the patent information for the actual coding, I also began working on the patent application for the physical handheld device.

Figure 7.6 is the conceptual design of how I envisioned the initial WAR-B device to look. It would be curvy and sleek, with the form factor of a small mobile phone. The front and back covers would be that of a stainless steel looking hard plastic, with a dense liquid crystal display.

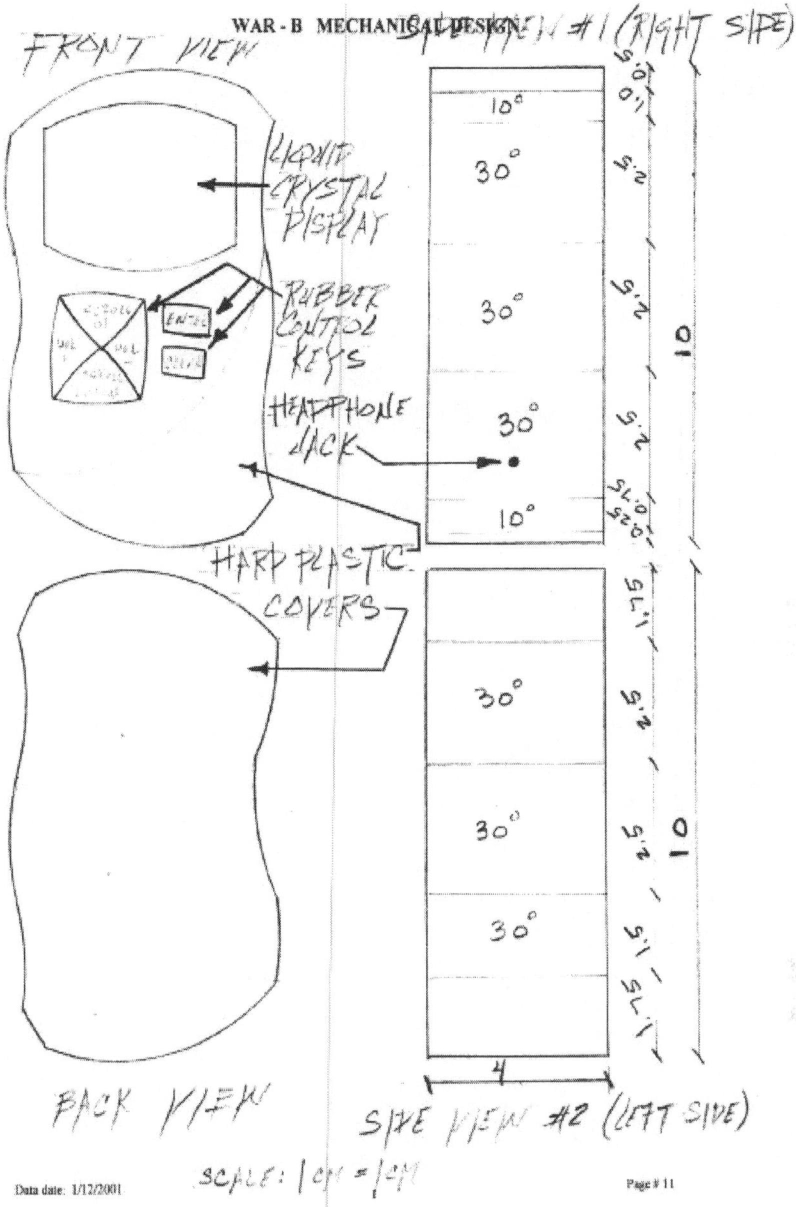
WAR - B MECHANICAL DESIGN
FRONT VIEW
SIDE VIEW #1 (RIGHT SIDE)
LIQUID CRYSTAL DISPLAY
RUBBER CONTROL KEYS
HEADPHONE JACK
HARD PLASTIC COVERS
BACK VIEW
SIDE VIEW #2 (LEFT SIDE)
SCALE: 1 CM = 1 CM
Data date: 1/12/2001
Page # 11

Figure 7.6

Figure 7.7 shows a hard lined drawing of the initial WAR-B handheld. Though the conception design was sleek and curvy, the hard line drawing gives a more accurate description of the actual area of the form factor.

Figure 7.8 shows the inside detail of how the mother board and circuitry diagrams were to be laid out.

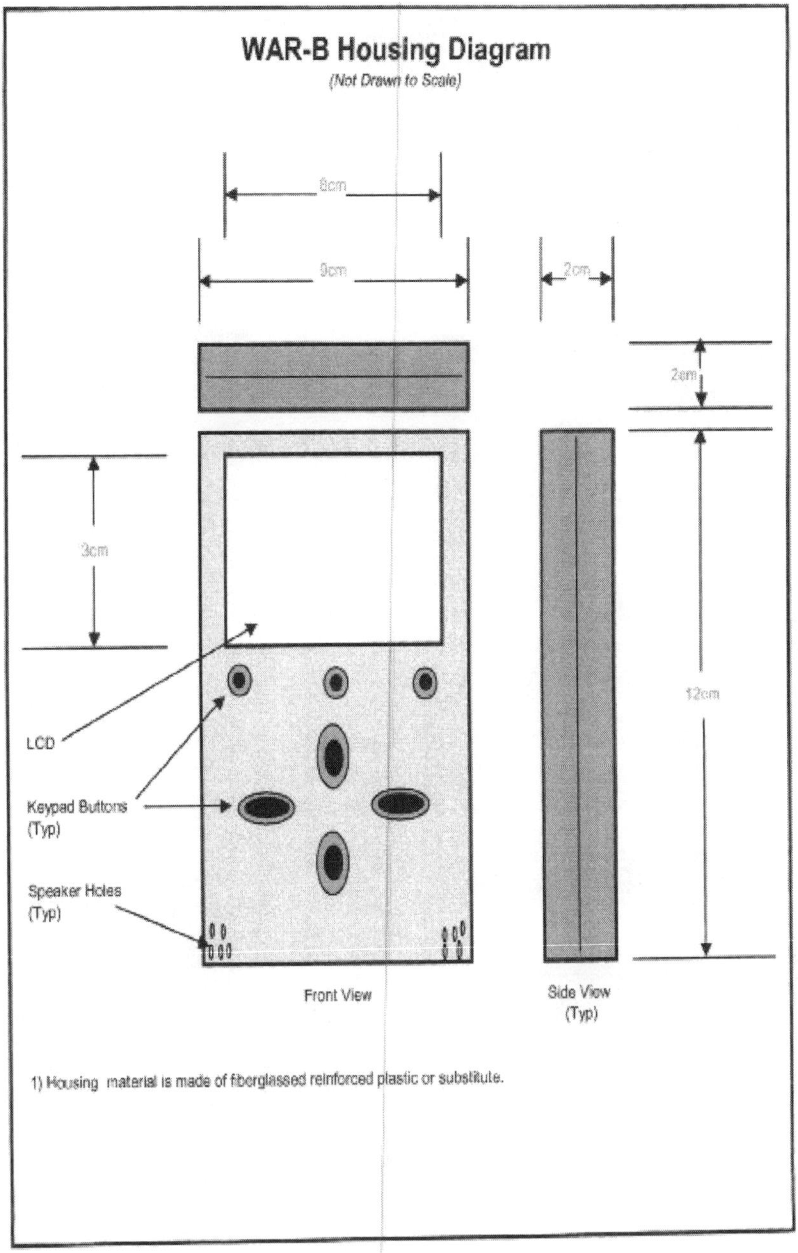

WAR-B Housing Diagram
(Not Drawn to Scale)
8cm
9cm
2cm
2cm
3cm
12cm
LCD
Keypad Buttons
(Typ)
Speaker Holes
(Typ)
Front View
Side View
(Typ)
1) Housing material is made of fiberglassed reinforced plastic or substitute.

Figure 7.7

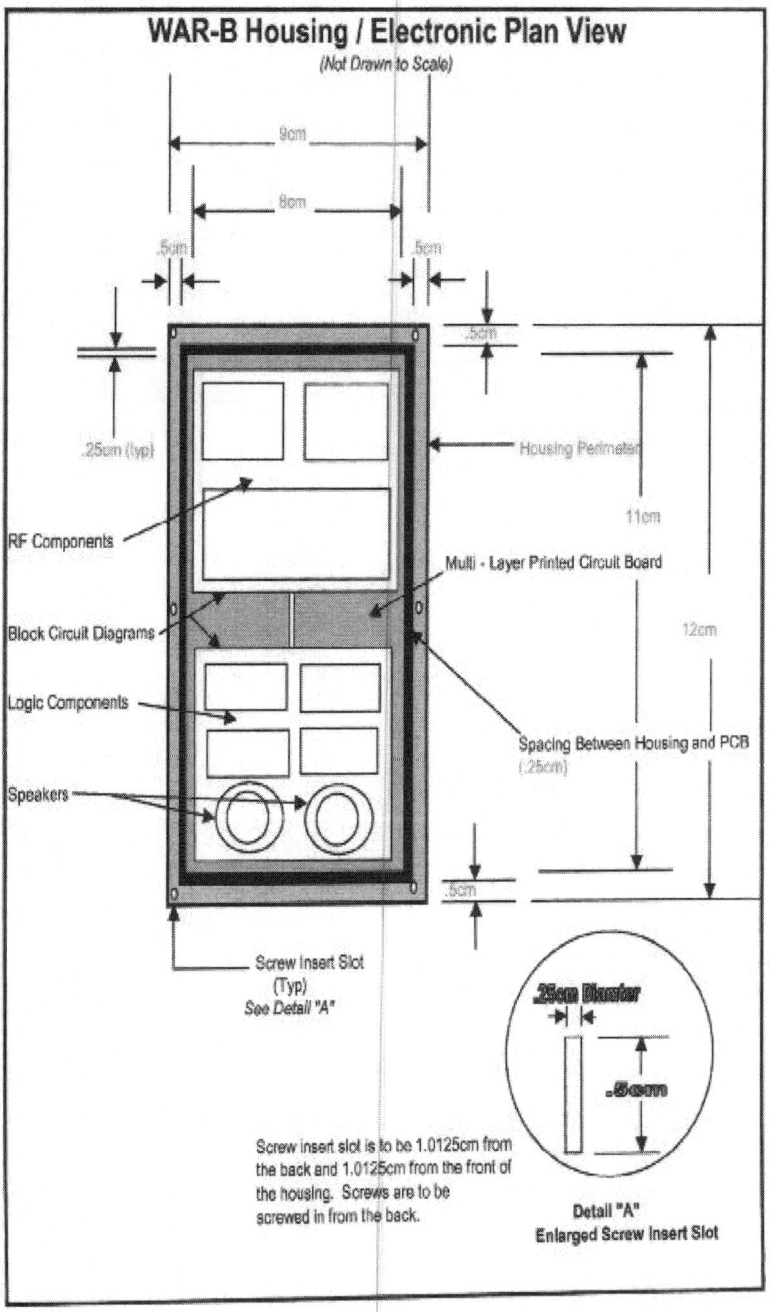
WAR-B Housing / Electronic Plan View
(Not Drawn to Scale)
9cm
8cm
.5cm
.5cm
.5cm
.25cm (typ)
Housing Perimeter
11cm
RF Components
Multi - Layer Printed Circuit Board
12cm
Block Circuit Diagrams
Logic Components
Spacing Between Housing and PCB
(.25cm)
Speakers
.5cm
Screw Insert Slot
(Typ)
See Detail "A"
.25cm Diameter
.5cm
Screw insert slot is to be 1.0125cm from the back and 1.0125cm from the front of the housing. Screws are to be screwed in from the back.
Detail "A"
Enlarged Screw Insert Slot

Figure 7.8

While working on the different patents, I also began reaching out to other national mobile phone carriers to attempt to schedule meetings to discuss partnering as well. This could allow me to have my code placed in their mobile phones.

Of course as I began moving forward with the major players, we all signed disclosure agreements that prohibited each from discussing the technologies with outside sources that we learn of each other's tcchnologies.

What I did learn was that the technology itself did not belong to the mobile phone carriers. There were third parties who created what are called the chipsets (motherboard units), that are placed in the phones. Those guys were who to whom the actual CDMA, TDMA, GSM and EDGE technologies belonged. The mobile phone carriers only built their wireless platforms on those technologies. Thus just as the wireless carriers were working with the technology distributers, I began meeting with them as well to have my code placed (embedded) into their chipsets. This would allow my code to be on the cell phones of all the carriers of which the technology distributors were selling chipsets.

At the same time, I began meeting with the manufacturers who created the actual skeleton (the part we see) of the mobile phones. After-all my goal was to create a hand held device that, would allow users to access radio stations around the country, anywhere at any time. With almost a year gone by, the concept of 3G was gaining ground. I knew that just radio could not be the only source of entertainment provided. Thus I began toying with the concept of television streaming.

I knew just by virtue of the relationships I had developed with the compression developer, that my code could stream a feature length film. However, I needed to do a little more research to see how to stream live television. What I learned was that video was divided in to frames.

Reflect back to the years of cartoon animation, you will visualize how there was a slow flicker as the cartoon figures made bodily movements. The faster the flicker the more natural the movements became. The faster the flicker the more the eye is deceived. Motion picture experts have helped us to understand the art of motion as it relates to animated images. There is a certain speed that that a flickering image can make (number of frames flickering per second), that could deceive the eye into believing that a segment of still picture frames is actually in motion if changing at a certain speed per second. The human mind visualizes true movement at the the magic number 24 frames per second.

Once the number of frames are changing at a pace of 24 frames per second, our minds begin to believe that there is actual movement. The more frames exceeding 24 per second, gives us greater detail of the movement. Thus a movie that is action packed can have hundreds of frames changing every second to give us the greatest of visual deception to make us believe that what we really see is movement.

These are some of the basic concepts that I had to teach myself in order to understand the technology that I was attempting to create. Generally when I have the best idea I have ever had, right now, my ideas consist of more than just what I am attempting to create.

Even if your concept is not as scientific as to create a new technological device, you still should have a very good understanding of the intricate details that can make your concept develop properly.

I can't express the importance of RESEARCH. In large companies, they spend hundreds of thousands of dollars per year on Research and Development (R&D). These dollars cover the cost of everything from human resources to testing and studies. You may say, "Dude, I am not trying to go that deep. I just want to start a business where I can sell paper products." OK. That is fine. But tell me this, where are you going to buy your paper? Are you going to buy from a local retail store and then resell it? Will your paper products consist of greeting cards? If so, are you going to create the greeting cards? Better yet, if you want to sell paper products, are you going to create your own paper? This may sound funny at first. However, I am willing to believe that if I could create a handheld device that could provide radio from stations around the country then you can create your own paper.

Whatever your idea is, do the research. Answer the questions before they are asked. In the past, libraries were good sources to do research. Today we rely heavily upon the internet. However, I believe that the perfect hybrid are the local bookstores. Libraries are great for historical data. But, the time frame between when information arrives in the library and when it is actually made public often times takes approximately three to four weeks.

The internet is a great place to research for the latest and greatest information on a topic. However, as you dig down into the information, you also have to dig through what is fact and what is the author's opinion on blog sites.

Periodicals found in bookstores can give you the greatest sense of in-depth research. Many periodicals are published bi-weekly and some even weekly. Definitely if your next best idea of all time is in the tech industry, this would be where you get your greatest amount of research accomplished. The tech industry is evolving daily. Of course the internet can give you an hour by hour update in real time. The periodicals can give you credible web sites that you can go to find such accurate and immediate updates.

Every greatest idea of all time needs to be protected. The Patent and Trademark Office (PTO), located in Washington, DC helps to facilitate such protection. Most patents provide protection to you for seven years. Simply put, you invent a widget. You get a patent on the widget. No-one can duplicate your widget and make a profit on it without your express written consent for seven years. After seven years, the competition will become fierce and you may begin seeing several widgets similar to yours hitting the market. This is often the case in the prescription pharmaceutical drug market. Once the pharmaceutical patent has expired, you start to see and hear about various generic drugs of a similar type.

Applying for a patent or a copyright is not hard; it is just paper work intense. Thus, if you know that you are not up for the challenge of completing a lot of paper work, double and triple checking your application for errors. You should hire a PTO professional. There are various agencies who claim to perform such tasks. However, many of them are only out to get your money. I have heard of cases where such agencies collect your money upfront and then start to avoid your phone calls. I have also heard of such agencies who swindle you out of one to three percent of all future earnings on the widget. This is done by giving you a warm a fuzzy feeling and not charging you up front to do the work.

The most effective and reliable PTO professional you can hire is a Patent Attorney. More often than not, they have put a patent application together and submitted it for a patent that is very similar in need to the one you are requesting. A Patent Attorney has a pretty good idea of what it is going to cost you to the complete the application and attorney fees. The application itself has a hard fixed cost as provided by the Patent and Trademark Office. However, there could be some variable costs that an application may require depending on the complexity of the widget.

When it comes to business decisions you make should have a contract for every occasion. This is definitely no different when it comes to intellectual property. Intellectual property today is often referred to copyrights of software.

However, it is not limited to software. The ownership of copyrights to images, music and videos are intellectual property as well. Music artists are those who are most often recognized as being imposed on when it comes to not totally owning his or her music and songs. Major record labels often request that ownership be signed over prior to completing big record deals. This protects the major labels from an artist taking her songs and leaving the label at will, while also taking songs and music produced along with them.

Many artists have become business savvy and have begun negotiating ownership of their masters. This is ownership of the master file that is published for copyrights. The initial record deal may be a lot less than what could have been negotiated. However by owning the master, it gives an artist leverage when negotiating other deals. In some cases a catalog of masters could be worth a half billion dollars. With that being the case, the masters become assets that can be leveraged for bank deals.

For most start-up business owners, owning music is not likely. But, owning images (pictures), is very likely. If you have a start-up business and you have hired a photographer to take your picture to be placed in magazines, on billboards and etc... Take note, you most likely do not own your own images.

When you set up deals to perform marketing photo and video shoots, you should always draw up an agreement with the photographer and / or the videographer to release to you all rights of images and videos taken. Otherwise you could pay for a four hour photo shoot and when you use one of the images on your own, you could find yourself being sued by the photographer. Yep, that's right! The photographer that you paid most likely owns the images of "your" likeness.

After concluding that technology had caught up with me and surpassed me in terms of WAR-B and the original plan for it, I transcended WAR-B into WAR-B Music. WAR-B Music was a predecessor for MyHipHopDepartment.com. It was a website I created to compete within the online movie video and video game rental business space.

Though the business was small, I made it a point to make sure that an agreement was put in place with all photographers that photos were released to me with all ownership rights. I requested ownership of photos from their most raw and pure forms to those with most detailed of touchups.

In either case, I wanted the right to all images so that if a "Best of WAR-B Photos" was ever released it would be coming directly from my camp and not produced without my knowing.

The Sassy Girl Photo Shoot was actually shot via video as well. Thus I requested both the photographer and the camera man to release all rights (in writing) to all photos and all videos of the shoot.

With full ownership I could use the images to market my current products. I could also come up with new and creative ideas and use those images to market those products as well. I could even go back to my days of TS Exposure and create a new, and hot, calendar.

With the video, I may want to create a making of the Sassy Girl DVD one day. Or, I may just want to keep it in a shoebox and sit on it. Regardless of what I decided to do with it, it is mine and I have total ownership.

Your ideas are your intellectual property. Protect them. Your logos, your designs, your computer codes and anything intelligent is your intellectual property. If you don't protect them, someone will steal them. Regardless of how cheesy they may sound, regardless of how bad your design, your photos or videos may seem, they belong to you.

CHAPTER 8

CORPORATE CHALLENGE

I was invited to speak to a very small group just a little while back. It was more so to speak with a focus group of managers of a Fortune 10 Company. Though we spoke on several topics, we touched on several topics that for some reason kept resurfacing. It was actually a pretty good conversation piece, especially since one of the participants in the group was one of my former managers in Corporate America.

The overall topic was *How to Keep a Self Motivated Employee Motivated.* I am sure you have run across this in a job description of a job posting. Every good manager wants to hire a "self starter." The problem is, when they hire someone that is a self starter, the person hired typically completes the tasks at more than doubled the pace of the average person who is not a self starter. When this happens, you get an employee with lots of idle time because even a good manager cannot keep them busy enough.

If you are this type of person, you can clearly relate, given that you understand because you are probably bored at work. Either you are going to pretend you are working or you are going to create new ways of making your company more productive. The issue I take with this is if you are pretending to be busy, you really are just wasting time. If you are being creative and using your ingenuity to make your position and your company more productive you are creating work that you will not get paid to do.

The average manager in Corporate America does not know how to deal with your talent. Actually you are viewed as a threat. Even though it was placed in the job description on the job board that "Person must be a Self Starter and able to work independently without a lot of direction," that is not exactly what the Manager is looking for or requesting. Those are definitions that Human Resources like to use to attract good talent. It would help if Human

Resources would communicate with Department Managers so that they could get on the same page as to for what they would actually like to hire.

Department Managers, typically do not want Self Starters. They really want someone that can "Manage their time wisely." If you can manage your time wisely, you can get your projects done, keep your manager out of hot water and not be viewed as a threat.

In Corporate America most are attempting to climb up the ladder. If you place your hands on the ladder where your Manager already is, you better believe that you will get stepped on. Corporate America is not the right place for an entrepreneur with fire in her lungs. I understand that everyone has to learn how to operate a business before they can start one. However, if you are working in the industry in which you plan, start a business, you should investigate potential restrictions.

The problem with this is Corporate America is cut throat. Not only must you "Be Ware" of those that don't want you to out climb them up the corporate ladder but, it is taboo to even think about competing with your company.

The first thing a company will do who feels their employees stand a chance to compete against them in the future is to have them sign a "non-compete clause." This restricts you from gaining access to sensitive information. It further eliminates you from thinking that you are savvy enough or even having the audacity to start a business that will compete against your current company.

The next thing that they will request is for you to sign is a "restrictive covenant." This is another clause that prohibits you from doing business in a certain area, or within a particular mile radius of the area in which you currently work.

Entrepreneurs can't stand the idea that they are being tied down. As an entrepreneur you are like a raging bull. As you are challenged by Corporate America to stay in the cage, your blood flow is pumping faster and faster. You are never going to be given the opportunity to demonstrate your true potential because if you do, you will be viewed as a threat on the rise with the title of the Employee Who Used to Work There.

This is true if you work for a major company represented on Wall Street or a small business with a store front on Main Street. When you were hired and told about all of the great opportunities for advancement, they forgot to mention that you should stay in your lane and only be a Self Starter when asked to start.

This should not be viewed as an issue but, an understanding. Understand your role and stay in your lane. You were hired to perform a task and not come up with your next best idea you have ever had. The task that you were hired to perform, is associated with someone-else's Dream and the best idea they ever had. It is not your Dream and you cannot Dream their Dream. So, don't try.

At the same time, you shouldn't get caught becoming a permanent player in their dreams either. You are a raging bull. If you get caught living in someone-else's dream, the potential for your relationship will undoubtedly become volatile at best.

Unfortunately I have seen this in many instances of those in the legal field, medical and dental professions. After finishing professional school with a very lopsided student loan, doctors face the obstacle of trying to get educational loans paid off as quickly as they can. The best case scenario as viewed at the time is for them to become an associate for an already established medical practice or law firm. The issue is the practice that in which they choose to associate in is also in the same community in which they have chosen to live, and would like to set up their practice someday as well. Most medical and dental practices require that an associate sign a Restrictive Covenant agreement. This will force the associate to not practice in the within a given radius of the current practice for a period of twenty-four to thirty-six months.

Thus as you can see, try your best to stay away from agreements like these that require you not build your business where you want to build your business. If you must work in a firm or a practice before starting your own practice, do so in a community at least four to five miles away from your ideal location. It will be much easier to work as an associate for a couple of years with a commute to work than it will be for you to relocate your home to an area that was not your prime choice, just to be near the practice that you have built outside of your restricted area.

What business owners that make associates sign Restrictive Covenants don't realize is that, if patients and clients who are being served by Associates want to continuing being served by the associate, they are going to follow the Associate whether they have to commute or not.

Those owners chose you to work in their practices and firms because they saw that raging bull in you when they interviewed you. They knew then that you were going to go out there, build business, and bring business to the office. Their hopes are that you don't take the business when you leave. Thus to discourage you from leaving they place work restrictions on you.

Those restrictions work for the average Associate, who is O.K. not having to go out and build new business. But for that raging bull like yourself, it doesn't work and it never will. So to save time and chaos, don't even put yourself in that position. If you must practice as an Associate to get your feet off the ground, do so in an area where restrictions will not prohibit you long term.

These types of restrictions are not limited to only those who are in the legal, dental or medical professions. If you are a Sales Professional and have intentions on starting your own business, this is something you should look into as well. Many Sales Professionals sign restrictions when they accept the positions and don't even know it. Read every page and every print on every page, before you sign or initial any paper work when accepting employment.

There are common cases that Sales Professionals are prohibited from any type of sales within a region after employment ties are severed. This could be a case where a Pharmaceutical Sales Rep leaves her company to start her own venture. The venture may be to place vending machines in offices. If the vending machines to be placed are initially in doctors' offices in which you built relationships selling the pharmaceuticals, this could in fact be a violation of your restrictions. So again, read every page and every inch of every page of all documents you sign or place initials. Otherwise you will find yourself hostage to the corporation in which you have severed ties.

CHAPTER 9

NETWORK MARKETING

When you are an aggressive raging bull, you will become a marked person for those who are trying to pitch their ideas. Why, because if you believe in their ideas and concepts you could help them make money.

I have no feeling either way good or bad, about network marketing. My only thought is this; if you don't want to be pitched in on the ideas, don't go to the meetings. If you agree to join a network marketing organization, crank up and go full throttle! Going at a half beat pace, will net you "0" gains and, waste a lot of peoples' time.

What is "full throttle?" That is a good question and I am glad you asked.

The first thing any network marketing organization is going to want you to do is put together a list of names and phone numbers of all of your family friends (Group A) who you communicate with on a daily basis. A good network marketing organization will also have you ask all of your friends and family to put together a list of all of their family and friends (Group B).

Once you have put your list together, the next thing to do is call each person in Group A, and let them know of the new business in which you are involved. Ask them if they would be so kind as to come to a mixer of friends so that you may be able to show them how using your new product could help them achieve certain goals, such as saving money on using your product as opposed to using the competitors' products that they may currently be using.

Remember Group A are those with whom you are directly associated. These are your relatives and very close friends. The odds of them telling you no, arc highly unlikely. However, buying into the concept of your new venture is unlikely as well.

Their group of friends, your Group B, is who you are really trying to bring into your network. This group is who Group A will invite to your mixer event, not because they are friends, but because they believe that is a group who would probably be interested in what you have to offer.

Typically when a new network marketing venture is introduced, there are two segments to the business. The first segment is the product itself. The Founder of the company came up with the best idea that she ever had, right now. In developing the idea she ran into a hurdle of getting the product placed. Thus, she decided to get her friends and her friends' friends involved in selling the product. The Founder agreed to give those who helped her sell the product a percentage of sales. She also encouraged her team to find new individuals who would like to make a little extra money.

Every individual that joined the team, they would be able to receive a portion of their sales as well. These individuals would all become a part of their team (or down line). Everyone would be making money. Those who were at the top of the Down Line would become success stories for the company that would be shared at regional and national meetings. Those at the bottom of the Down Line would view the successes of the others as a measuring stick to show they too could reach the top if they met the required performance.

The most confusing part of network marketing is whether to market the product or market the business opportunity to other entrepreneurs. By marketing and selling the product, you are building product awareness and brand exposure. This is actually the original intent of the Founder. She had an idea and, she wanted it to be launched. Her idea was the widget. She chose to network market, rather than traditional marketing.

However the network marketing phase is what most individuals feel is the easiest way to make the type of money that want to make. Their idea is if they can go out and find those who are willing to sell the widgets, they can make money from what those solicited sell, rather than attempting to try and sell the widgets on their own.

The problem arises when; an individual has his mixer of Group A and Group B. Those who sign up to be a part of the business then go out and try to attract team members by having a mixer of Group A and Group B. At this point, it becomes a cycle of having mixers and attracting individuals who want to be a part of the business rather than trying to have mixers to promote the actual widget.

After a point, everyone involved in the Down Line become a mere Human Resource Department for the business rather than Salesman of the business. The end result, the only money being made is through fees associated with becoming members of the business. In this type of Down Line, no one will make any real money.

If you choose to join a network marketing organization, and you want to be successful, your primary goal should be to actually get out and hustle to sell the product. When you have your Group A / Group B mixers, focus on selling widgets rather than trying to get individuals to sign up and join your Down Line so that you can recoup your fees you paid to join the organization.

When your friends see that you really have a genuine interest in selling the product, they will ask the tough questions to see if it is something they are interested in as well.

Your close friends and family, in Group A, are going to be a tough sell. They know you. They have seen your other ventures and business interests come and go.

However Group B only knows you through association, if at all. But your Group A, felt they may have an interest in what you are selling or, what you have to say about the business. You will probably get one member of Group B to join for every three members of Group A that are in attendance at your mixer. When they ask you about joining the business, you should focus more on the advantages and disadvantages of selling the widget as opposed to becoming a member of your Down Line. If they can believe in the potential of the product as much as you do, becoming a part of your team will inevitably happen.

If they are sincere with wanting to know more about the business and are hungry to join, they are going to corner you before the meeting is over and insist on getting more information. It is at that time you slide them your business card and, exchange contact information with them. Schedule a meeting with them within a week that includes your Team Leader. Let your Team Leader sell them on the concept of becoming a part of the business. This will give them a true sense of the business. This will allow them to have a feeling of being involved in the business and, it not just being just another sales job or pyramid scheme. You have sold her on the fact that you believe in the product so much that you were willing to sell the widgets as a means of building your business and making your money. By speaking with the Team Leader, she now understands that one of the perks of being in the business is that if someone wants to join, she can sign them up and receive referral dollars that could eventually reimburse her sign-up fee and more.

If you send out the message at your initial mixer that you are trying to sign up individuals for the businesses and, a lot of money can be done doing so, you will in fact sign up individuals. As they sign up, they will have mixers and they will sign up individuals. The cycle will continue, and your entire Down Line will be of individuals who are signing other's up with no one doing any selling of the product. At the end of the day, everyone will be making their money back on what it cost them to join the organization, but no one is making real money from the residual sells of the products.

When you begin selling your product, you should stay in contact with your clients. Most network marketing opportunities provide some sort of residual income. This is an income that you will receive weekly or monthly for as long as your client is using the services or purchasing the product. If your client discontinues the service or the purchase of the product, you will no longer receive payments. Thus you should create lists of your clients and provide a monthly maintenance service to them. That is calling them, send them an email or a text message. Ask them, what do they think of the product? Get feedback good or bad. Remember this is network marketing. These are individuals with whom you have direct communication. If you are continually asking pros and cons of the product, they will most likely continue the service. Thus you will not lose residual income.

To really increase your business, you should ask your clients to host mixers for you. Remember that initially these clients were a part of either your Group A or Group B Network. However, you should now move them to your Group C Network. This is a very important part of your network! Your Group C are current clients. They are your best referral base. Their close friends and family are not merely Group A and Group B. They are Group 1A.

You ask what the difference between Group A is and Group B from Group 1A? It is simple. Group A and Group B was a stab in the dark of individuals that may or may not sign up. Group 1A are the associates of the Group C. Ordinarily they would be classified as Group A or Group B. However they have seen the results or heard a great deal about the product from Group C, your current clients. They are approximately seventy-five percent sold on the product prior to you even saying a word. For this particular mixer, you should be prepared for more advanced questions from participants. After-all, these guys have somewhat been educated by Group C. If you are extremely knowledgeable of your product, you will be looking at an approximate seventy-percent success rate converting this Group from 1A to C before leaving the mixer.

As you become more and more educated about your product, you should begin to develop your presentation to present as a Team Leader. If you are successful, you better believe those around you will want to know what you are doing and how you are doing it. Your Down Line will grow. You will become a Team Leader. Your Down Line will be sending individuals to you to present how to become successful in the business. There are no tougher questions, than from those who are trying to understand exactly how they can make money, how hard and how much time it will take for them to get to the level in which they can realize their American Dreams.

Networking marketing is not easy. Done properly, it is not quick either. It takes time. Most network marketing organizations have it designed so that you do not need a full business plan, however you do need to be business minded and have a written strategy of how you are going to grow your business.

Before signing up for a network marketing organization, do your homework. Research the company. Find out who the Founders are and how long the company has been in existence. Get anunderstanding as to whether you are to receive your compensation via a paper check or if it will be automatically deposited into your bank account and how often.

If the opportunity sounds too good to be true, it probably is. If you can't find any real historical data on the company or the founder, there probably is none. If the Agreement (Contract) is too long to read, it is too long to sign.

Do your research.

CHAPTER 10

BUYING INTO A FRANCHISE

The concept of network marketing is based on business franchising. It is very simple, a person with a vision builds a successful business and she is willing to share her vision with others who are visionaries but don't want to spend the time researching the intricate details of making a business work. Therefore, they join forces with someone who has a proven success plan in making a particular business venture work.

Just as in network marketing, you will have to pay a fee to join the business as a franchise member. This is what is called a franchise fee. Unlike network marketing, to become a franchise owner is all about the product that has been developed. Your mission is to sell the widgets that the owner has developed and in the manner that the owner has developed.

Franchises have very strict specifications as to how a franchise owner is to build its business. With such strict specifications come training provided by the organization that teaches franchise members exactly how the business is to be operated. Product can only be purchased from specific vendors. Signage can only be installed by specific installers. In most cases construction of the store or restaurant can only be built by specific contractors.

These specifications make it easy for the end consumer to be guaranteed that a product purchased at any franchise location will taste the same or perform the same no matter what franchise location the product was purchased.

The fee to become franchise members is often times very costly. I have seen costs to participate in known successful franchises go from $10,000 to $1.5 million. Of course you can find franchises that are ten percent of that and, you can find franchises that are ten times those amounts. However, those numbers are relatively the average costs.

The benefit of joining a successful franchise is that everything is already in place. All of the guess work has been taken out of the equation. If you have a question you are a phone call, text message or an e-mail away from getting your question answered rather quickly.

The down side to joining a franchise is that you must adhere to the rules and guidelines of the franchise with no deviation. You can't add one more pickle to your burger because it makes the burger taste ten times better. You cannot give your customer another 10 minutes of car wash time because you are attempting to exceed customer satisfaction. Any deviation from the franchise standards and you could be in breach of contract of your franchise agreement. What does this mean? The franchise owner may be able to come and seize your property. Thus be very careful when investing into a franchise.

In most cases researching the opportunity of buying into a franchise is much easier than researching a network marketing organization. Most franchises are publicly traded companies. This means that the information that you need to research is available through reports that have to be presented each year. These reports are compiled in what is called an Annual Report. The Annual Report, gives a bird's eye view as to what the CEO and his team deem as the most beneficial to the company for the share holders to make money. Thus if this is what the shareholders need to make sure they have their money invested in the appropriate business, you should be able to use it as well. Obtaining this report is very simple. Go to the company's website and you should be able to find this information under a link titled "investors."

As you research the franchise, flip to the financial statements. See what the top line (Gross Revenue) is and compare to what the bottom line (profit) is. It is your decision as to whether or not you want to invest, however you should understand how to read the financials. Please understand that a business that has a large amount of revenue coming in annually does not make it a successful business. The same business can have a large expense line as well, which means profit is not that great.

Nor does it mean that it is the best business for you just because the profit line is great. This business could have a franchise fee that exceeds what you have to invest in a business. Or, a small amount of expenses were incurred in the previous year(s), which may call for a larger expense line in the coming year(s). As you can see, that large profit may have been a one-time hit.

Very creative individuals are able to get their hands on large sums of cash in order to purchase a franchise. However, most successful franchises require more than cash in order to become a franchise member. They require different levels of net worth. I have seen net worth requirements as low as twenty-five thousand dollars and as high as 1.5 million dollars.

By requiring members to have certain levels of net worth, assures the franchise owner that in tough times, and there will be tough times, that you will be able to leverage your net worth to make decisions that will see your business through economic crisis. After-all, at the end of the day, the franchise owner wants your franchise location to succeed. If you succeed, the franchise itself is viewed as successful. If your business fails, the franchise is viewed as a potential risk to other potential investors.

A franchise also looks at your liquid assets. These are your assets that are easily convertible to cash. Of course this will be a part of your overall net worth. However, it is viewed separately to determine how quickly you can access cash.

Hard assets such as real-estate are viewed as well. Even though real-estate is viewed in your overall net worth, a snap shot of real-estate is taken to determine how much cash you may be able to convert from real estate in a relatively short period of time if needed. Converting real-estate into cash is relatively tricky. Markets vary from state to state and even city to city.

Your available credit line is also a key component of attaining a franchise. Franchise owners want to know, how much cash is available to you from lenders. These lenders could be credit card companies or conventional lending institutions.

Remember it is not how much credit you have, it is how much credit is available to you. You may have a $100,000 credit line. But, if you only have $5,000 available to you, the other $95,000 is irrelevant.

When buying into a franchise, always do a business to business deal and not a personal deal. For instance, say you want to open a Jimmy John's Hamburger Restaurant franchise in Atlanta. Create a company such as Food

Companies Unlimited, LLC (FCU). Rather than you purchasing the franchise under your name, purchase it under the name of FCU. So the company that owns the Jimmy John's Hamburger Restaurant in Atlanta is FCU.

Buying a franchise is a very lofty business dealing. Never go buy into a franchise without the assistance of a good attorney and a good CPA from the very beginning. If a business is being franchised out, you better believe that the corporation has already done everything legally possible to cover itself, its assets, and the reputation of the franchise. If you do not prepare yourself and your business as well, the odds of you having a very rocky road ahead is most certain.

Please understand that if you meet all of the necessary requirements to purchase a franchise, you are more valuable to the franchise ownership than purchasing the franchise is to you. So, as soon as you know that you qualify to do the deal of purchasing the franchise, pull the reins back a little. Slow down the pace of getting the deal done.

This is going to be the total opposite of what the franchise owners will be attempting to do. As soon as they know that they have a qualified individual, they are going to try to get the deal done as soon as possible. The reason why is because, they don't want you to get "buyer's remorse." That is to start having doubts and second guessing whether or not you are doing the right thing by making such a large investment.

Thus, you should slow down the pace of getting the deal done. Take a second and third look at all of the literature that you have read while researching the company. Spend a few more sessions with your Attorney and your CPA. Ask them if there are any items that you may be missing or overlooking. Request a list of franchise members that you may be able to speak with one on one and get their opinions, both pros and cons, of opening a new franchise location. Once you feel comfortable with all of the information that you have compiled, pick the pace back up and get the deal done.

Understand that getting the deal done is only the beginning. This is your business. Buying into a franchise allows you to utilize the systems that have been set into place for you to get a jump start on opening your doors. However, you must be proactive in locating top talent to work your store. You must, identify the local marketing venues that will allow you to spread the word about the coming and the opening of your store. You must know the projected revenue, expenses and profit of other franchise members to gauge the realistic expectations and successes of your store.

Every type of business in every industry has a franchise. Whether you should become a franchise member or start your own business without a franchise association is purely a judgment call. Most business owners who become franchise members do so because they do not want the headaches of trying to determine all of the pieces of the puzzle to make the business work. The franchise gives them the ability to use the cookie cutter recipe to be open for a business in a relatively short period of time. They also, like the idea of having someone to fall back on, that they can call, if they have questions. It is almost like having an experienced partner without really having a partner.

On the other hand, you have what I call the self-publisher. This type of business person is the hardcore entrepreneur. She wants to do things her way and is not up to being placed inside of any type of box. She wants to create the business plan, the marketing plan and determine with what vendors she does business.

She may have a large amount of capital to play with or none. She may have a high net worth or again, none. Regardless of her financial status, having money or the lack thereof will not stop her from opening her business.

She does not have to have the permission of the franchise owner to be able to open her business in a particular location. However, she probably has pulled the annual report of local franchises in the industry that she wants to build her business and has developed strategies on how to compete against the franchise in specific areas.

This type of business is what most large companies, franchises, would call a Mom and Pop Shop. It is hard for franchises to market against a Mom and Pop Shop. The reason why, is because they base their marketing and advertisement on community, relationship and family. The Franchise, many times, will only allow you to market in ways that are franchise specific. Thus, you will not be able to tie your business relationship to the community as the competing business can. So as you weigh opening a Mom & Pop Shop versus buying into a franchise, be sure to check the temperature of the area in which you are looking to locate, to determine how the community may receive your business.

CHAPTER 11

BIG CITY

One opportunity that I was taking a look at required me to determine whether or not to buy into a franchise or to build a Mom & Pop Shop. The venture was that of a beauty and barber salon. I called my two cats who were my go-to guys for business ideas. After a few months of researching the concept, we decided to move forward.

We developed a marketing plan that had a target market of 18-30 year old African-American, White and Latino males and females. Thus, we had to identify a location that could meet the demands of such a diverse geographic location.

I remembered from a Business Marketing class, years before that, when one of the country's top fast food chains was interested in opening up new store locations they simply opened up in an area where its primary competitor was already established. The reason for this, was because it would not have to utilize the financial resources and human resources to determine if a location was ideal or not. The established fast food chain had already done the work. By establishing the successful presence, it was a no brainer that the similar chain could be successful as well.

Thus, we began researching franchised barber and beauty salons. Our goal was to find out in what types of locations they were building their business and what was the demographic of their clientele. What we found was that most of the franchised salons were in indoor malls. This made a lot of sense to us once we realized it. The foot traffic was second to no other type of location.

Guys have you ever been walking in the mall and a female with black body pants caught your eyes? As your girlfriend slapped you upside your head for your total stare down, you noticed that she went inside the beauty shop or the nail salon? Of course not! But, yep that is where she went. The black body fit pants is the signature marketing mechanism for the indoor beauty and nail salons.

When a female gets her hair and nails done, she wants to feel like the total package. She also wants her stylist to be the total package. The black fitted pants gives the ambiance of a stylist who can make you look as good as she looks. Since it is the ambiance that attracts guys as well, he will bring up a conversation to her to see if she has ever gotten her hair done in that salon. Even though she has never thought of getting her hair done there, she now has a question. "Did he see someone come out of there that has a hair style that he likes? Hmmm... Maybe I should try them out." It is just that simple and voila, now there is a beauty salon in the mall that is banging, and not because of the females that sought it out but, the men who saw someone go in.

However as we looked for locations, we knew that indoor mall location would not be within our budget. However, we looked for outdoor strip malls and shopping centers. We called the Planning and Zoning Offices of cities that we had interest in and requested data of traffic surveys at various intersections. We researched the anchor stores to determine how long they had been operating at specific locations. We also monitored traffic in the parking lots of shopping centers that we were interested in opening a salon to determine what type of traffic was coming in and out of the location.

Now if we were to have opened a franchise instead going the Mom & Pop Shop route, all of this research would have been done for us. It would have just been a matter of deciding what location would be best for us. In the same breath, the corporate headquarters would have told us where we could open as opposed to us deciding to open in our own desired locations.

Also if we were to buy into a franchise for the salon that we were researching, we would have to come out of $30,000 that would have included a franchise fee of $5000 and a "turn-key investment" of $25,000. That is, $5,000 would have been our membership in the club to call ourselves ABC Beauty Salon. $25,000 would have covered cost for us to complete construction build out, get a certificate of occupancy and the keys to walk right into the salon space ready to do business.

In addition to have a "turn-key" business, we would have had support from the corporate headquarters for marketing information. With a recognized brand name behind the business, less emphasis would have had to go into marketing the name of the business. When individuals were to notice that we were in the community, the brand name itself would have driven the traffic to our location.

Corporate would have also sent a representative down, to negotiate the terms of the lease for us as well. The locations that we were researching went anywhere from $6 per square foot to lease to $30 per square foot. If we would have gone with the franchise salon, odds are we would have been able to save five to seven percent on monthly lease cost. So, there are some great advantages with going with a franchise.

The down side to going with the franchise is almost twenty-five percent of gross profit would have gone back to be paid to corporate in forms of marketing, legal and other franchise fees. After, we created our financial statements and pro-forma we realized that if we didn't join the franchise that we would gross approximately twenty percent more in revenue per month if we allocated expenses in the same form as were being designated as fees by the franchise.

We would have to be accountable for the line items as opposed to Corporate being accountable. However, we decided that every little bit of earnings would help.

We believed that if we had the ability to open a franchise store, we could channel just a little bit more of our energy, do a little bit more grunt work and open up our own Mom & Pop Shop Salon.

After six months of researching, negotiating leases, shopping for barber / stylist chairs, developing relationships with hair product distributors, contracting out the construction and hiring barbers and stylists we opened up Big City Salons!

Again, this process would have been a whole lot simpler if we would have just bought into a franchise. However, the bonding with my business partners and the learning experiences would not have been the same.

We don't think we did too shabby of a job when negotiating the lease with the development company. They wanted $30 per square foot for the 1,100 square feet store-front space. The first thing to understand when negotiating a commercial lease is how much you are being charged per square foot. $30 per square foot for 1,100 SF calculates to be $33,000. This number is divided by twelve to give you the total amount that you will be spending per month. Thus the lease that we were presented would have been for $2,750 per month.

Now if you are doing real quick mental math, you are probably saying to yourself “If those dumb dumbs would have bought the franchise, they would have already saved $3,000.”

Figure 11.1

Figure 11.2

That would not be a bad assumption but, it would not be accurate. $30,000 would have gotten us a turn-key deal thru the lease, construction, and open to do business. We would have even saved maybe seven percent on the lease amount. That would have had us at $30,504 for a monthly lease a savings of approximately $2,500. The reason, why I am giving you this specific information is because the lease was not included in the franchise fees. All that was included and is normally included in the franchise fees for most franchises is the fee to be a member, the cost to complete construction and get your doors open.

So, if you are looking at opening a franchise, understand that the fees that you are paying will get you support, marketing and brand recognition but it does not include your lease amount for whatever lease terms you have.

The space that we negotiated was a space that had been vacant for a few years. A major sandwich franchise anchored the shopping strip with a national mobile phone carrier having a space in the shopping strip as well. The strip had apartment buildings to the North, South and East and was located on a drive area to the West with a major intersection where over 100,000 cars passed thru daily. The apartment complex was made up of mainly young adults, both males and females (African-American, White and Latino) in the age group of twenty-one to thirty-five (our target market). We had found a prime location!

But, back to that lease, the development company wanted $2,750 per month for a space that had been vacant for more than three years. What we believed was the development company wanted us to take on the lease more than we wanted to open up a beauty salon in that location. So, we came up with a plan and presented it to the development company.

Our plan was simple. We needed to build out the space to our liking. In order to build out the space we would have to enter into a lease agreement for a specified period of time. The plan we presented was that, we would enter the lease agreement only if we could the get the first nine months of the lease waived so that we could complete construction without paying lease while under construction. We also wanted the lease amount to be $15 per square foot.

Of course, the nature of a business to business relationship is for both sides to win. This is the old Win-Win! Of course we didn't get everything that we wanted but, we do feel like we received a Win.

We didn't get nine months free lease, but they gave us six months. We didn't get the $15 per square foot lease but, we did get $18. That came out to be $19,800. Yes, that is right. We negotiated a savings of over $13,000 on the annual lease.

Buying into the franchise would have saved us approximately seven percent on the lease. However, we saved approximately fifty percent doing it ourselves. Now, let's keep it real. Of course the franchise guys had a heck of a lot more experience than we did in negotiating leases. They may have gotten us a real good rate in a more prime location but, I think it would have been real tough to out-perform the negotiations that we finalized.

CHAPTER 12

REAL ESTATE

The one industry all entrepreneurs have in common is Real Estate. Either you are going to choose to do business in some form of the Real Estate industry or, you are going to make some very important decisions as to where you will locate your business. Either you will build a building, lease an office or you will choose to work out of your own home. In either case, one of the first decisions you will make in regards to your new business will involve Real Estate.

The real estate game is a gangster business. It is an industry that can determine the fate of entire economies. So, understand that those who are good at it, eat steak. Those who do not do well at it, don't eat. When you decide to participate in the real estate game, you should first become well versed in the area you are attempting to attack. In every area of real estate there are vultures watching you set up major deals. They are the same vultures hoping that you die so that they can swoop down and nibble on your heart as your blood turns cold.

When you are involved in any real estate transaction, you must remember that it is all business. There is nothing personal about it. Though your deal may begin with a win-win for all parties involved, the truth be told, only one party will win. If you get caught lunching, the other side will eat you alive.

Because Real Estate dominates the entrepreneurial markets, there are several different industries that you can enter under the real estate umbrella in which you can join many who have become extremely successful.

As you drive around neighborhoods of most of the major metropolitan cities in the United States, you will see homes that are up for sell listed by Real Estate Agents. Becoming a licensed Real Estate Agent, is a matter of taking Real Estate

Classes and passing a rather rigorous exam that varies from state to state.

A Real Estate Agent works under the authority of a licensed Real Estate Broker. Agents are required to work under a Broker for a specific period of time. States average approximately two years for an Agent to work under a Broker. I consider Agents to be one of the first layers of the Real Estate & Construction Industry. A good agent knows her local market very well. She knows what is selling and what is not selling. She knows the communities that are growing and, she knows the communities that are not growing and why. A good Real Estate Agent has all of the answers for her clients. If she does not have the answers, she knows where to get them fast.

Since Agents work for Brokers, they normally officially work out of the office of the Broker with most of the work being conducted either out of their home or their automobiles.

The biggest part of being a Real Estate Agent is communicating her contract to her client effectively. Most Real Estate Contracts are pretty much cookie cutters. The boiler plate is standard. It is when the negotiations begin that verbiage communications is extremely important.

If you think that the negotiations in a real estate deal ends with how much a Buyer is willing to pay and, Seller is willing to take, you are wrong. That is not where it ends, that is where it begins. Think about it. Say you want to buy a property. The property costs $350,000. Do you ask the Seller to change the color of the carpet before you agree upon a price? Or, do you ask that the parking lot be repaved prior to signing a contract? Odds are, probably not. Typically a buy / sell price is agreed upon and, then the negotiations begin as to what things are contingent upon happening in order to close the deal.

Real Estate Agents are usually restricted by law as to how much they can charge to complete contract negotiations by the state in which they are licensed. Agent Fees are normally discussed in terms of Points. Points are percentage points of the real estate closing cost to complete the deal. Percentage points average six to seven percent. That is, if an agent closes a $500,000 deal, there stands to be $30,000 to $35,000 in Agent fees included. Some states require that the Buyer be represented by a Buyer's Agent and, that the Seller be represented by a Seller's Agent. This reduces the odds of one Agent representing both parties convoluting a transaction. However, some states do not require brokerage firms representing both Agents. Thus you can often find a Buyer's Agent and Seller's Agent working under the same Broker to complete the deal. Agents, normally have a fee that they must pay to the Broker per transaction. Therefore, the six percent fee in the deal can be a lot less for the Agent. Both Agents will split the six percent. They will then pay the Broker maybe one-percent of their earnings. Thus, the Broker will be getting paid on the buy end and the sell end of the transaction.

This Broker / Agent Relationship is merely network marketing. The more Agents that a Broker can attract, the less of the actual selling of real estate the Broker will have to perform. The Broker is held accountable for all contract language and negotiations initiated by her Agent. So, she must make sure that her Agents are as prepared and professional in their business transactions as possible.

It is close to impossible for Agents to know every house or commercial building that is going up for sale or lease in a particular area, therefore the more successful Agents conduct their business in specific areas. Real Estate Agents call this farming. The available properties, within a specific area are your farm. A good Real Estate Agent wants to control the entire farm. Thus, they are constantly passing out fliers and business cards in the local community. This allows them to advertise that they are the go-to Real Estate Agent in the community.

When an Agent conducts an Open House, one good way to advertise for it is to send out invitations to as many of its surrounding neighbors as possible. Most people know someone who has inquired about moving into their neighborhoods. The local neighbors may show up to the Open House and they may not. But, if they will tell someone who is interested in relocating, that may be the one person who purchases the home that you are trying to sell.

However, taking on the entrepreneurial role of becoming a Real Estate Agent can become very exhausting. After-all, every agency has several agents who are attempting to farm the same territory as you are farming. The larger brokerage firms have hundreds and even thousands of agents located in specific farm areas. This can make becoming successful at being a Real Estate Agent frustrating at times.

To be a successful Real Estate Agent, you have to always be on the cutting edge advertising you and your business. You should attend local neighborhood association meetings and introduce yourself. Most individuals who are actively apart of neighborhood associations, are the nosy neighbors. These guys are good to have on your speed dial, or better yet to be on their speed dial. They know who is looking at moving out of the neighborhood. They know who wants to move into the neighborhood. You want these guys to call you as soon as they get any idea that there is about to be a real estate negotiation potentially going down.

You should have an interactive website. You should attend business breakfast meetings of other local business professionals. You should be overly social with social media marketing.

Market your business and partner with Building Contractors. Building Contractors, especially Home Builders often times build spec Homes. These are homes that are models of what they build. Home Builders love to work with good Real Estate Agents. This allows them to build homes and not have the pressure on them to get the home sold.

If you can get a new construction home sold prior to the home being completed, you will rise right to the top the list of the Real Estate Agents that Home Builder will use when trying to get a home sold.

Join local business groups and associations. There are many local business groups that meet for breakfast one day per week to discuss how to network and do business transactions together. Go to those meetings. Introduce yourself and request more personable one on one lunches and meetings with attendees. Sooner or later, you will find that you will be a part of Who's Who in your farm area.

Your primary human resource should be Mortgage Brokers. 90% of Buyers use some type of financing when purchasing a home. Buyers tend to seek financing prior to seeking a Real Estate Agent to search for homes. If you have good relationships with several Mortgage Brokers you will receive business funneled to you by the Mortgage Brokers.

You may have been trying to find a business to get into and have attended a few real estate seminars put on by real estate gurus. So, you may be actively building business in real estate without really having a license. This is a very tricky way in which to participate in this industry but, it is being done.

Most guys who are doing business this way in Real Estate are not bound by conventional rules of real estate. You are able to use some very slippery concepts that allow you to conduct business in a manner that is most gangster. For instance, you go out and find a property that is for sale. You then approach the seller and put an offer in on the property. In your Real Estate Contract you make the deal contingent upon you receiving financing for the deal within sixty days or longer. If the Seller agrees, then you go and find someone who wants to buy the property. In some states, understand that it is illegal two have to contracts on two properties at the same time. However, you can "assign" your contract to the new buyer.

You name the price. Let's say your original contract price is $500,000. You have not received financing for the deal so, the deal will potentially go dead. You inform the Seller that financing is not looking good. However at the same time, you let her know that you don't want to kill the deal because you know how important it is for her to get a fair price for the property as soon as possible. You tell her that you have someone-else who is more prepared to close on the deal than you are at this time. However, they are looking to buy at $475,000. Your Seller agrees. You then go to your potential Assignee, and inform them of the sell price. If they do the deal thru you, they can get the house at that price. If they don't do the deal thru you they will have to pay the $500,000. Your offer to them is that they pay you a $5,000 "finder's fee" and, you assign the contract over to them. Your Seller makes her money, your Assignee saves $20,000 and you make $5,000 with no money down. Incredible! This is a very tricky game to play, but if you do it right you can buy and sell properties with no money down!

The Real Estate game also involves the lending industry. Mortgage Brokers act in the same capacity as Real Estate Brokers, to their Loan Officers. These Loan Officers go out and find business just as Real Estate Agents. They farm their areas and the network with local neighborhood associations, home builders and local business people to try and build business.

The process to becoming a Loan Officer, is very similar to becoming a Real Estate Agent. Each state has classes that must be taken and an exam that must be passed. After that, the Loan Officer must find a Mortgage Broker to sponsor her and work under for a year and half to two years, depending upon rules and regulations of the state in which they are working.

After the apprenticeship period is completed, the Loan Officer has the ability to take the Mortgage Broker's Exam to become a full-fledged Mortgage

Broker. In some states, a Loan Officer is able to take the Mortgage Broker's Exam rather than the Loan Officer's Exam. Once the required amount of time has elapsed, all the Loan Officer has to do is update her license from a Loan Officer to a Mortgage Broker. Otherwise, if she took the Loan Officer's Exam, she will have to take the Mortgage Broker's Exam as well in order to begin functioning in that capacity.

Several states require their Real Estate Agents to take Mortgage Broker classes. However, they do not require their Mortgage Brokers and Loan Officers to take the Real Estate courses. Thus it is very possible to become a Loan Officer and a Real Estate Agent simultaneously. As well as, it is very possible for a Real Estate Broker to be a Mortgage Broker as well. However, there is a lot of room for grey areas and conflicts of interest. If you are not very sound in your understanding of rules, regulations and laws set forth accordingly for both segments of the industry you could find yourself in violation of white collar criminal activity that will have your home temporarily relocated for ten to twenty-five years, on some uncharted island with personal security and your meals prepared timely.

CHAPTER 13

THE MAKING OF

In the past few years leading up to the year 2006, the US Economy has seen record highs. The rich have gotten richer. The poor seemed to actually have a chance to believe in the American Dream. My Dream like many other entrepreneurs was to get rich and live like the rich.

Finding a good job at that time was easy to do, especially with a Masters in Business Administration. But, finding a job was not what I was looking to find. I was still in search of the business idea that would lead to receiving a phone call from some multi-billionaire that would ask to buy my idea for $1 billion.

I had been a lot of places, met a lot people and seen the good and bad of business deals. But, like many others, my motto was "get rich or die trying." So my pursuit of my American Dream was still alive and kicking.

Whenever I meet someone or listen to someone speak, my goal is to take away at least one positive thing from that person. At one of the seminars that I attended, I had an opportunity to hear possibly the most powerful business motivational speaker of my time. I don't remember everything or even most of what he spoke about. However he did say one thing that I have taken with me for the past twenty years. He spoke about a concept of "Automobile University." This was a concept of when you are in commute to work, pop in an audio book and maximize your time commuting. This would be listening to something other than just to the radio.

As I began listening to audio books, I found myself more and more intrigued by the business giants who all seemed to dabble into Real Estate.

With my chosen career path in Construction Management, by default, I had a great deal of knowledge, more than the average bear who was trying to enter the Real Estate arena. Most others who were trying to get a foot in the door were going the Real Estate Agent route. However, as I started to speak with more and more aspiring Real Estate Agents and Brokers, I found myself answering some very common questions and providing resources for those who were looking for good plumbers, electricians, and air condition contractors.

As these Real Estate Agents got deeper into their entrepreneurial ventures, they found themselves purchasing properties. Some began to flip properties. That is, they, would buy them as cheap as they could, below the current market value, throw a little paint on them, lay down some new carpet and sell the properties as close to market value as possible.

Now you may be asking yourself why someone would sell a good property for cheap, if all they have to do is paint it, put down new carpet, and then get more for the asking price. It is simple. Not everyone selling a property is in it for the business. Most sellers need to sell their property. They may be racing against having their property foreclosed. They may be relocating to a new city, state or even country. The Seller may want to upsize or downsize, and selling her property can relieve the stress of having two mortgages. Regardless as to why a seller would be willing to sell at a lower price, sometimes a good deal can stare you right in the face.

Initially I became the “go-to-man” for all people looking for good contractors to work on their properties. Then, I became the “go-to-man” for all contractors looking for work.

Thus, I decided to start providing services for a small finder’s fee and consulting fee. Now that my services were no longer “free,” and I wanted a piece of the action too, the request for referrals began to dwindle. After a couple of years of referring contractors and business, the referral both ways saw a plateau. I initially thought to myself that business was a good run while it lasted.

However, just as a baby lion in the jungle that has made his first kill, I had tasted blood. I saw how much money Real Estate Agents were making on quick flips by making some minor repairs. I couldn't just walk away without trying to get a piece of that pie. After-all, they needed good contractors. They were coming to me. I had a service that was demanded but, did not realize how to produce to the demand.

As I researched becoming a Real Estate Agent and, researched the necessary classes and schools to get certified, I ran up on a Real Estate Broker who also was a Mortgage Broker. I began to tell him how I had been working with Real Estate Agents and that now, I wanted to become a Real Estate Agent so that I could buy, fix-up and flip my own properties.

He thought that would be a good idea as well. As a matter of fact, he indicated that he could have it set up so that I could get work under his license once I passed the Real Estate Test. Even more so, since he was Mortgage Broker as well, I could also work under his

Mortgage Broker's License if I decided to take that exam.

I am more of a numbers guy and, the Mortgage Broker's Exam, dealt more with the actual financing and contract volume of a real estate deal than the Real Estate Exam. Plus, I could immediately take the Mortgage Broker's Exam after completing the required courses within ninety days. So, that's what I did. I became a license Loan Officer within a relatively short period of time.

Upon doing so, I contacted the guy to see how we could make the deal work for me to work under his licenses. When I contacted him, he seemed to be more excited than I was. We scheduled a meeting and, I met with he and several of his top Loan Officers the following Saturday morning at his office.

He mentioned that he had recently purchased the office building and was in the process of doing some major upgrades. The purchase was through a deal that he had conducted through a business to business transaction. I wasn't exactly sure what that meant but, he seemed to be pretty excited. According to him everything had been aligning properly and his business had been seeing drastic jumps in growth.

After meeting with he and his associates for several hours, we then broke away and met one on one for approximately another hour and a half. This is when we really started to hash out how to make our business relationship work. All I really wanted was a Mortgage Broker who would sponsor me for the next year and a half while I worked to become a licensed Broker.

However, what I was presented with was something much more than an opportunity to become a Mortgage Broker. What I was offered, was a partnership in a new division of his company. Just as I was interested in working with him to gain the sponsorship needed to become a licensed Mortgage Broker. He, just as other Real Estate and Mortgage Brokers, wanted to access the knowledge that I had to build his Real Estate Portfolio. In essence it was a “Quid Pro Quo.” He would sponsor me as a Loan Officer, and I would develop a construction department within his company.

In return, I would receive two points on all mortgage deals that I brought to the table and closed. As well as, I would receive forty percent of all profits on all construction projects. Within six months, we had approximately $2,000,000 worth of residential construction under contract.

Within the term of this agreement, I began calling on some of my old commercial construction buddies, informing them that I was back the construction game but this time on the residential construction side.

I also began calling on some commercial construction material vendors. Though pricing was very similar to commercial construction, some vendors had different prices for residential builders than for commercial builders. I needed to understand my cost options, as well as my finance options. In some cases, I was able to get better pricing as a residential builder however, I was able to get credit and better terms as a commercial builder.

Within approximately three months of us finalizing our agreement we had broken ground on our first deal. It was about a half million dollar custom home. My part of the deal was to get it built as quick as possible with as much quality as possible. Figure 13.1 displays our ground breaking home as it was closed in.

Closing in a construction project is to get the project to a level in which the outer shell is completed. Contractors strive to get their project to this level of completion because it allows them to continue work on the inside of the project and, bad weather conditions do not pose a potential threat to slow the project down.

On all of my projects, whether construction or mobile telecommunications engineering, I like to have multiple tasks performed simultaneously. This allows for the project to be completed as quickly as possible without risking the project's integrity. In Figure 13.1, you will see that the brick is on-site and ready to be placed and the shingles are on the roof and ready to be placed. What you are not able to see is that rough plumbing and rough electrical phases are being performed inside of the home.

This home was built slightly outside of the city limits. This is both good and bad. The bad part is that subcontractors were not governed by City Building Inspectors to complete their work in manners acceptable to local building codes. Thus, I had to hire a building inspector independently to see that my contractors were held to the same level of workmanship as they would have been had they been working several miles away inside the city limits.

On the other hand, since the home did not reside within the city limits, I was able to push the project along at a much faster pace. By hiring an independent inspector, I was not forced to wait on the schedule of the city's Codes Department to send out an inspector at every phase completed. We were able to coordinate having multiple phases inspected simultaneously. Thus a project that would have taken six months to complete, we were able to complete in four and half months.

What makes a TLR Custom Home different from other custom home builders is the amount of standard detail that I place into my chore projects. All of my homes are built with granite counter tops throughout the home as a standard. Rounded corners are a must. Very detailed crown molding throughout the home is found in all of the homes that I have built. All of my homes are prewired for surround sounds and have pre-built areas ready for outdoor kitchens. The stair rails have iron spindles. The first floor is of stained concrete, to give you the grand floor effect. See Figure 13.9.

Most builders like to throw in one upgrade that will give a buyer the impression of wow! I like for the entire home to give the WOW effect! This makes a potential buyer feel as if he is getting a bigger bang for his buck.

I look at it like this, if I put an additional $9,000 in the construction of a home, I will increase the appraised value before sale by $45,000. Thus my cost to build the home in Figure 13.1 was approximately

Figure 13.1

Figure 13.2

$224,000. The appraised value was approximately $380,000. The standard upgrades increased the value to $425,000. The math was real simple.

Figure 13.3 displays the north wall of the game room with masonry being installed on the counter of the wet bar area. You can also see the South wall of the game room and its interior designs of custom paint colors, crown molding and high ceiling.

Figure 13.4 displays the iron spindles with oak hand rails. It also displays the home entry with a royal arch entry way and massive double doors.

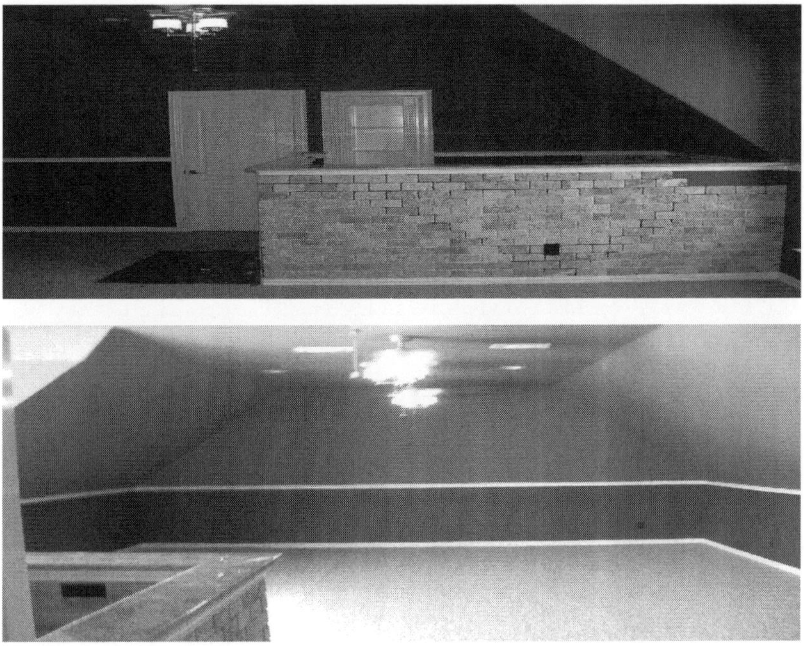

Figure 13.3

Figure 13.4

Figure 13.5

Figure 13.6

Figure 13.7

Figure 13.8

Figure 13.9

Thus to take advantage of all options, depending on which suppliers I was work with, I may have applied for credit as a residential builder or I may have applied for credit as commercial builder.

In order to understand your options, you must ask questions and then listen to how your question is answered. Please note that I said "listen to how it is answered," not to what is the answer. Good sales people know how to phrase their answers. They sell for a reason because, they are good at what they do.

As I built credit accounts with the vendors, my partner secured the land deals and secured buyers. He used his access to the MLS Listing Service as a Real Estate Agent to locate good properties to purchase. He used his ability as a Mortgage Broker to get the buyers financed.

I very quickly realized that, the value that I was bringing to the company was incomparable to what the company was offering me. Thus as it became more and more clear, we decided to dissolve our business relationship and part ways after our initial contract had reached its term.

I learned a lot in that business relationship. I learned a lot about doing business in the Real Estate game, as well as in doing business with people in general. However, the most important thing I learned in that relationship was something that I had remembered from my old Business Law Professor. That is, every good business will come to an end. Always create and exit strategy when creating a new business or business relationship.

Whether you create a business with someone you know or, create a business to business venture with a business that you don't know, you should always create an exit strategy. Even though every idea is The Best Idea You Ever Had Right Now, it is more than likely going to someday hit a ceiling with no chance of bouncing back one day. A business plan is not complete without an Exit Plan.

Give your business goals to achieve. These goals are more likely going to be financial goals. If your business misses its goals on a regular basis, that is a sign that you may need to think about revamping your business plan or setting the stage for your Exit Strategy.

However goals don't necessarily have to be directly financial. You may know that there are some major players in your industry. You figure that if you can create joint ventures or Business to Business relationships with those businesses that you will be able to establish your business as an up and coming player in the market. Give your business some dates. If you are not able to adequately create partnerships and ventures with those companies, you should have time frames set into place to start making your way out of the business.

I was able to realize some financial successes in the residential construction game. But, my greatest success has to be credited to the Exit Plan that I had in place when I entered my initial agreement with the Real Estate / Mortgage Broker.

CHAPTER 14

GOOD HELP IS HARD TO FIND

Building your dream business is almost impossible to do alone. In order to grow your business, it will be essential for you to identify good sources of labor. Employment Agencies are often great places for you to find readily available help. It is best to find an agency that caters to the needs of your specific business. This will allow you to hire an employee with a very short learning curve. New hires that come from such agencies will often have the necessary experience to come right in and go to work, with a relatively short learning curve.

In the age of the internet you can also find literally thousands of potential contractors that you can hire to work for you or partner with you to be politically correct. However, beware that if a contractor submits you a proposal that seems too good to be true, it probably is.

Contracting is not just for homebuilding or construction projects. You may want to start a Home Health Care Business. Thus you may be able to find nurses to contract with you from online websites. If you really have skills, you may want to design custom automobiles. You may be able to find a drafter, a mechanic or supplier for your parts to build your custom cars.

When I come up with new business concepts or consult with individuals in regards to finding labor or contractors, I like to ride around and collect phone numbers on automobiles of businesses that are conducting mobile advertisements. The reason I like to do this is because, these are business owners that are demonstrating a desire to grow their businesses. Usually these are small business owners and, they typically are willing to give you really good deals to win your business.

Regardless, of how you obtain your contracted sources, always conduct a background check. It is good to get a list of three to five referrals from the potential contractor and make phone calls to determine how their business relationships began, how they carried out their promises and how they have followed up since the job has been completed.

Of course, the referrals that they give you will be the best referrals that they have to offer. Thus, you should expect nothing but positive feedback. When you are interviewing the contractor, you should ask probing questions and find out past customers that are not on the list of referrals that they provide. Contact those referrals and, see what type of feedback they may provide.

Just because, a past source may have negative feedback, does not mean that contractor is not a person with whom to conduct business. However, the more information you can gather, the better you will be able to predict how the contractor will respond to your needs under various conditions.

At, the same time, just because you receive positive feedback does not mean that the potential contractor does not have any character flaws. For instance, the contractor may perform great work but, she may be a "non-morning person." Thus she may be late coming in every morning. Her work may be extraordinary. However she may be the type of person that likes to rebut every suggestive action that you ask her to take.

Therefore, you need to know who you are hiring before you sign the contract. Otherwise, you may run up on a contractor who understands the power of an iron-clad contract. Then, you will realize that it is easier to enter an agreement than it is to get out of one. Or, you will find that to get out of a solid contract could become relatively expensive.

I have been a party on both sides of the contractor to contractor relationship. In either case, no matter how the contract language reads, I always include an "arbitration clause." This clause simply allows all contract disputes to resolve in arbitration and not in a court of law.

When creating an arbitration clause, you should be very specific. You should note very specific details of the name of the arbitrator (or firm), the city, county and state in which the arbitration will be conducted.

I like arbitration as a legal route for various reasons. One, if you find yourself going into a court of law to settle a dispute you can start racking up court costs in the tens of thousands dollars rather quickly. Arbitration should be a lot less expensive. Your arbitrator has a fee. That fee should be detailed in your contract. It could be $50 per hour or $250 per hour. Your contract should list how fee rate increases will be taken care of by both parties, if the fees do increase.

Your contract should detail the rules of arbitration. For instance, the rule can be that arbitration is not to exceed “X” number of hours. If a resolution between both parties cannot be met, either you can set the next rule for the arbitrator to make the final decision or, you can then elect to go into a court of law.

Once you have threatened legal action or, have legal action threaten against you, you will then know that you really have a business. Arbitration keeps you out of court, at least for a time.

But, you should always have your attorney review your contract documents. The more iron-clad your contract is initially, the better your chances of not having to come off of as much money when legal disputes arise.

CHAPTER 15

BUSINESS ENTITIES

Another cost that should be taken into consideration is your filing fees. Every state is a little different. I have seen cost vary from $35 to $350 to file for your businesses with state agencies.

The type of entity you create is going to dictate how much or how little it is going to cost you to file. There are several major entities that you can create for your business. The more common one is a Sole Proprietorship.

This entity is very simple and, usually just requires a very nominal fee. Typically with this entity all you have to do is create a Doing Business As (DBA) with your local city municipality. This is a business that is operated by an individual. It is very simple for individuals with small businesses to create Sole Proprietorships. They are inexpensive and very quick to get your business up and operating. An example of a common name of a Sole Proprietorship could be: *Erica Simon Doing Business as Yum Yum Cookies and Creams!*

The next business entity is a Partnership. Partnerships, just as Sole Proprietorships are simple and inexpensive to create. When two or more individuals create or, are in business together, they generally have a Partnership. An example of a common name of a Partnership could be:

Erica Simon and Paul Simon Doing Business as Yum Yum Cookies and Creams!

If your business has the potential to demonstrate early growth, you may want to establish your business entity as a Limited Liability Company (LLC). An LLC is filed with the Secretary of State of the state in which you are doing business. The filing fee is typically more expensive than filing for Sole Proprietorships and Partnerships. An example of the name of an LLC is: *Yum Yum Cookies and Creams, LLC!*

If your business is a partnership and you believe it has the potential for early growth, you may want to form a Limited Liability Partnership (LLP). This entity is also filed with the Secretary State of the state in which you are doing business. The cost to file an LLP is typically the same cost as it is to create an LLC. An example of the name of an LLP could be: *Simon & Simon, LLP.*

Though the Sole Proprietorship is the most common form of business, the corporation is the most common that we know about. The corporation, typically the C-Corp (big business) is what we see in businesses that we patronize. A common name of a C-Corp is: *Yum Yum Cookies and Cream, Inc.*

There are pros and cons to creating each of these entities. However, we will discuss the pro and cons of each later. Right now it is just important to understand that this is a cost associated with forming your entity. For those in your World, your idea becomes a business when you create your first prototype or sample. However, once you create and file your entity with the appropriate local municipality or state, your business is then recognized as an official business.

Does your idea require a copyright, patent, trademark or service mark? This is an expense for which you should immediately prepare. Copyrights are relatively inexpensive to file. On the other hand, patents, trademarks, and service marks are a little more in cost. These costs range from $25 to $500. Copyrights, patents, trademarks, and service marks are all filed with the PTO in Washington, DC. We will discuss in greater deal about this later as well. However, just remember if you need to protect your idea, put this line item cost near the top of your "to do list."

I am more of a self publisher than most. This simply means, if there are any line items that I can perform on my own, I prefer to do them myself. However, I do realize that because of the number of ventures in which I have been involved, I am able to use the resources of my mental repetitions of creating businesses to self publish as opposed to hiring out contractors to perform certain functions.

For example rather than filing your own entities, many prefer to hire someone to perform the entity filings. In most cases, you may want to hire an attorney who specializes in this area, or hire a business consultant. The cost to hire someone to perform such services could range anywhere from $500 to $2500. This is in addition to the actual filing fees. Though this sounds like a lot of money, if you know that you are not good at following through with a lot of paperwork, you may want to go this route. It could save you a lot of time and save you even more money in the long run.

LLC's, LLP's, Sole Proprietorships and Corporations are what I term as simple company structures. These types of companies are for profit companies. Depending on the entity, the Internal Revenue Service tax codes govern how the revenue of the business is taxed.

Another type of business is a non-profit organization. By creating your business as a non-profit you will be able to receive sponsorships and financial donations from other businesses that will be 100% tax deductible as charitable contributions.

The good thing about creating a non-profit organization is that some major corporations have full departments that look for legitimate non-profit organizations to partner with to make financial contributions.

Locating these departments in most cases is just a matter of contacting the Public Relations Department and asking for the person in charge of charitable contributions.

The downside is that most major corporations already have non-profit organizations in which they invest funds. Such non-profits' partnerships allow major corporations to gain national exposure for giving back to the community. It is a win / win for both. The major corporations receive a certain amount of free publicity from the giving. At the same time, their giving is recognized as write-offs by the Internal Revenue Service (IRS).

It takes a well put together marketing plan to target corporations with charitable contribution departments, in order to get them to begin donating to new organizations.

You are able to establish simple business entities within most states. However, to create non-profits that will allow your sponsors and donors to receive tax-deductible contributions you must file for a 501-C3 with the (IRS).

After coaching several seasons of youth sports, I realized a need for financial assistance for some of my players for uniforms and registration fees. I also began to provide additional training and conducted camps for children around the metroplex. Many of the children could not afford the registration fees, thus by creating a Non-Profit 501-C3, I was able to receive some contributions from sponsors.

The sponsors were not major corporations, but they were local community businesses. By partnering with my organization they received free positive community publicity. My organization received the ability to provide scholarships to players who ordinarily would not have been able to participate in our skills and drills camps.

CHAPTER 16

PREPARING FOR GROWTH

Though marketing is the biggest logistical challenge that young and start-up businesses face, adequate financing is why those same businesses do not succeed. Some of you may say "duh." However, this is not as simple as it sounds.

Many start-up businesses have enough financing to start the business. However properly budgeting to maintain the existence of the business until it becomes self sustaining is a whole other story. Your budget should be priority number one.

Of course you should create a budget that is common to your business type. However, the most important thing is to create a budget in which you have a full understanding. If your budgeted numbers are too high or too low initially, as long as you know where the over-runs or under-runs are, you will be able to adjust accordingly at a later point.

Many start-up businesses that qualify for small business loans start out by requesting too little money. Once the loan is received, within a relatively short period of time the loaned funds are depleted. This begins the cycle of the business chasing its tail every month in order to make good on the bills and the loan payment. With just a few more dollars requested on the front end, a start-up business could buy just enough time to get its finances in the black. There is no one particular type of business that is less susceptible to having funding issues than another. Neither is there a business that is less likely to need a good budget from which to operate.

CEO's and COO's of major corporations make approximately ninety percent of their decisions in some shape or fashion based on a budget number for departments within its organization. For instance, companies hire and fire based on projected budgets. Companies make capital expenses or, avoid making capital expenses based on budgets. Companies even plan to have or not to have meetings, based on projected budgets.

Simply put, your budget is your guide, your measuring stick. Create as solid of a budget as you can initially. This will help you be able to determine if you are or are not on the road to creating a profitable business, or tell you what you need to do in order to build a self-sustaining business for the future.

However, just like a rule, there will come times when the budget is broken.

Most start-up businesses fail within the first three years of existence. My theory is start-ups fail within the first three years, because they do not have effective budget planning in place. A start-up without a budget is like driving a car without a destination.

As you conduct your research, be sure to jot down every time you run across an item that can be an expense to your business. Ask yourself, will you run your business alone? Or, will you have an Administrative Assistant, Office Manager, or Project Manager? Determine all of your potential costs and categorize them. IE: They may be admin cost, supply cost, marketing cost and etc... Create a budget for each of these categories and build your business around your budget and, not your budget around your business.

Though most start-ups fail, of course there are those that do not. The lack of finances is the major reason why many dreams do not get off the ground. Inadequate financing is why most start-ups are not able to succeed. Believe it or not, not being prepared for financial growth and success is why the next level of businesses self destruct.

Yes that is correct, your business growing too fast or, just growing and you not knowing what to do with your profits, could be the demise of your business. A small business that has witnessed some successes, should prepare to not do business as usual. It should look into building up its human resources. Small business owners wear many hats. They are the Marketing Director, the Lead Accountant, the Vice-President of Technology and if they operate out of their cars like most, they are the Administrative Assistant.

Thus as your business is advancing to the next level, be prepared to hire personnel that knows more about subject matters than you do. Or, just be prepared to train someone to take over different roles and responsibilities to free up your time so that you can focus your attention on other areas.

You should create based on needs and, not based on what you think a business like yours should look. You may need to be ready to hire a Project Manager (PM). However, you may only need a good Administrative Assistant to begin scheduling appointments, taking your calls and even acting as your PM or Assistant PM. As your business grows, you can relieve some of her duties, elevate her to PM or VP and hire her some help when needed.

How about if your business begins to triple its monthly revenue on a continuous basis? What do you do with your additional income from this revenue? After you have exhausted the needs for human and capital resources, you then may still realize a substantial amount of extra money in your bank account. It is not good to leave large sums of money in an ordinary savings account if you are not going to have immediate needs for liquid assets. If you have money that you can afford to not touch for at least three months, you should begin exploring other means to saving and investing those funds.

Rather than letting your money sit in a traditional savings account, you may want to ask your banker about interest rates of their money market accounts. Money Markets tend to gain approximately 1.5 to 3 percent more in interest than traditional savings accounts. Money Markets are low risk investments. The downside to a money market account is that, you are not able to withdraw from your assets for a minimum of ninety days.

A certificate of deposit (CD's) is another good low risk financial investment that you can make. CD's have interest rates based on the federal government's prime interest rate. Many CD's will have an interest rate based on the prime rate plus one or two percentage points. For example, the prime rate may be 5.1 percent. Your CD may have a guaranteed interest rate of prime plus 1 (5.1% + 1%= 6.1%). This is definitely higher than a traditional savings account and, even most money markets. Again, the downside is that your funds are not readily accessible to you. CD's have durations that they must be invested before you are able to cash out. Typical durations are six months, one year, three years and five years. Longer durations, yield greater returns on investments.

A typical very safe investment is the purchase of government bonds. They are low risk and they normally guarantee a high rate of return over a long period of time. The way government bonds work is that you make a purchase in US dollar denominations and, you are guaranteed a specific dollar return on your investment over a period of time. An example of this is you purchase government bonds with a face value of $10,000, in seven years you will be able to cash them in for $20,000. Again, this is very safe investment. However, your money will be tied up for seven years.

As an investment novice, you may or may not be aware of money market accounts, CD's and government bonds. However, when we think of investing we naturally think stocks. Investing in stocks is a very high risk investment. Unless you have time to watch your investments on a daily basis and, maybe even an hourly basis depending on your investment, I don't encourage young business people to heavily invest into stocks. There are some very positive upsides to investing in stocks. They can have extremely high levels of return. You can also cash out of your stock investments at anytime during the trading day giving you near instant access to your investment. The downside to investing into stocks is that they can lose money just as fast as they make money. Stocks are volatile. They are worth only as much or as little as investors trading them in a given day.

The investment that I encourage young business owners to mainly invest their discretionary income is mutual funds. Mutual Funds are mid-level risk investments. Mutual Funds are actually a family of particular types of stocks. For instance, one mutual fund family may be stocks of ten paint companies. The value of the fund is not determined by one stock, but by an approximate value of the combined stocks. Thus, one of the stocks in the family may be losing money, but another stock in the family may be making money. Because mutual funds are families of stocks, they tend to show positive returns on investments over a thirty-six month cycle with an eight to ten percent return. Investing in mutual funds will allow you to play with a slightly riskier investment, but cash out when you need. At the same time, you may hold out for greater returns over a longer duration.

There are hundreds of Mutual Funds from which to choose to invest. Some funds are more risky than others. Funds are categorized under specific types of fund families. Treasury Bill Funds are funds comprised of government securities. These funds are less risky than most funds, more secure but could provide a lower rate of return.

Fixed Income Funds are combinations of bonds, debentures, treasury bills and mortgages. They are low risk and the returns are traditionally not very high relatively speaking.

Equity Funds are funds of traditional stocks. These funds can be categorized as Large Cap (major corporations), Mid Cap (mid-sized companies) and, Small Cap (small business).

Special Equity Funds are funds of several types of mutual funds such as real estate and precious metals.

Dividend Funds are preferred and common shares that pay above average returns.

Global and International Funds consists of money market securities of international companies.

It does not take a rocket scientist to learn how to invest your money. Neither does it take a "Financial Planner" at a rate of $750 per month to tell you where to put your money. If your business is now making $30,000 additional per year and you are paying a planner almost $10,000 per year to invest year $20,000 you may really need to be sitting on your earnings until your earnings is 10% of what you are paying someone to invest.

Otherwise, you can research the companies and funds on your own to determine where you want to invest your money. So when you do start paying a planner, you are able to ask them what they can do for you that you cannot do for yourself. You will then be able to maximize your investments while maximizing what you are paying to a Planner.

I once invested $2,000 into a company stock that yielded a return of $5,000 in less than two weeks.

A good rule of thumb to see that your investments are diversified is to take your age and subtract it from 100. This is the percentage of your investment that you should invest to high risk investments. The remainder you should split up among low to medium risk investments.

CHAPTER 17

THE CONCLUSION

So there you have it. This is My Story. This is My Song.

In 1990, with a couple of friends I started Tri-Set Enterprises. Little did I know that the journey to create a female of Color swimsuit calendar would be the basis for my song. As we departed back to our individual institutions of higher learning that Fall, we all three continued to pursue our individual passions. Friend Number one, received a degree in business and is now in upper management for a major US Firm. Friend Number Two, is now a licensed airplane pilot and is flying the friendly skies for a major US airline.

Me? Well, my story continued as I introduced the concept to my new business partner in the Spring of 1991 on the campus of Tuskegee University. To be honest, I actually thought that ride was over. I thought it was fun the summer before, attempting to make a twelve to six-teen month calendar of nothing but Beauties of the Week just like on page 43.

However, my new partner had struck up new ideas of how to make it happen. It was great! My interest was his interest. As we began to talk and speak more, we found that we had a lot in common. We both grew up in the homes of our grandparents. Our mothers were both named Carolyn. We both were from the South (He from Alabama and me from Arkansas). But, what really made the TS Exposure Calendar work was the biggest thing we had in common. We both had good eyes for fast cars and fine women.

We recruited models from on campus. We received major community buy-in and support for our efforts to borrow swimwear and receive sponsorships. We sold a few calendars. We didn't make a mint. However, we did well enough in an industry that did not have very much African-American involvement that gave us an even greater hunger to conquer new heights.

In the Fall of 1995, we started Kamatè. For me this has been my most fun and most rewarding project. When starting a business, the hardest groups of individuals to get to buy-in to your idea are friends and family. We knew we were on the right track with Kamatè when we started going out with friends and they were wearing our gear. I have even had a Kamatè sighting in recent weeks (over 15 years later). We had a website before most major corporations. We met many celebrities while building the brand. We were even celebrities ourselves in certain small circles.

We shut Kamatè down officially in the Summer of 1999. After four years, we had concluded that we were not in route to grow the business if we were to continue on the current path. That path was, we both were working in Corporate America and we were living in two different states. We felt that in order to grow the business, we needed to be in the same state and at least one of us needed to be taking on the business full time. But, it was a pretty good run. After making tens of thousands of dollars and spending tens of thousands dollars, traveling from Dallas to Chicago and New York to Las Vegas, it was over.

However the show did not stop there. In the year 2000 I came up with the concept of Wireless Access Radio Broadcasting (WAR-B). I was offered a six-figure sum to purchase WAR-B by a major communications company. I believed that the value of WAR-B was far greater than the amount offered. The deal was offered during a time when new laws were being discussed and passed as to how to control radio music over the internet. Thus, a "take-it or leave-it" type of proposal was presented to me. Yep you guessed it! I left it. To this day, I still believe I did the right thing. There is no way I would be able to sleep with myself taking less than what I believed it was worth at the time. Within ten years, a market that was not even known by many of those that are now working in it, is a hundred billion dollar industry. I have heard about too many instances in which artists were robbed of their dreams by taking peanuts from major corporations just to say that their music was on the air or, they were in a movie. That was not going to be me.

I discontinued my research of building the business in 2002. I locked away all of my documents. I sometimes pull them out now and then as, I compare many of the technology devices that are being sold to what I had designed ten years prior. I have even purchased many of the devices. However, everytime I pick up the devices, I just smile. I always see several components that those devices are missing. I know that I have those components already designed and, know exactly how to integrate them. I know that it is just a matter of time before they hit the market designed slightly different.

In 2003, we created Big City Beauty and Barber Salon (me and my two Business Partners). Our unique salon met the needs of African-Americans, Caucasian Americans and Latin-Americans. With such diversity within the salon, came the need to intervene with the barbers and stylists' insensitive conversations that they often would find themselves engaged in with their clients.

Also, since neither of the partners actually perform services of the salon, we found that we had to stay around the salon as much as possible to make sure the business was not being misrepresented (IE: the workers were really coming to work and, no drugs were being trafficked).

In 2005, we were presented with an offer to sell Big City to a small group. The deal made sense and we sold Big City.

While building Big City, I was also working on building a web-based company, MyHipHopDepartment.com. With Kamatè, we had designed our gear. However, I knew there were designers out there, just like we were, looking for a venue to sell their gear. Thus, I contacted those designers and negotiated deals with them to sell their gear over the internet. I was able to carry several brands that already had major commercial presences, as well as carry many independent designers.

Just like with Kamatè, this type of business took on visibility. Many music artists trying to get their CD's, and clothing designers trying to sell their lines main stream were wanting to meet with me. Most times, this also included their photographers, models, music producers and DJ's. After a while this became a headache. I just wanted to sell clothes and music on the internet. I didn't want to discuss with a whole entourage individuals as to why I should sell their gear.

So, I dropped many of the lines and kept a few, mainly those that already had brand recognition. I revamped the site, and added some advertising through Affiliate Marketing Programs. I bumped up the amount of advertising that I was doing for the site and, couldn't believe the amount of money that was generating just by Affiliate Marketing advertising.

I found web traffic increased when I began to offer music, videos and video games for sell. I slowly pulled out of online fashion and, I ramped up in those areas. Web traffic increased, thus the amount of money made advertising my Affiliates increased as well.

In 2006, I was able to take some of my earnings and invest in the real estate market. After partnering to build a few custom homes, I decided to do it alone. The home building market was great and the money was even greater. I figured the only way I could not become a billionaire in the industry would be if the American Economy collapsed. By George, it did! I had gambled the farm on real estate and construction and loss.

I had stacked all of my chips, financial and human resources that I had earned over the years to enter the greatest industry of all. In two years I made more money than I could have ever imagined. In two years and one day, the ride was over. The banks had frozen up lending to small builders and, all of a sudden there were as many homes being foreclosed on, as I was building and had under contract. The American economy was going down the tank and it was taking my business with it.

Though that deal was done, I still had the internet (MyHipHopDepartment.com) business. To be honest I was a little depressed and really did not care to put the time into monitoring the progress of the site.

I had actually used some of the funds from building the homes to create a line of female athletic and swimwear apparel, as well. I called the line Sassy Girl Fashions. I hired the best photographer and modeling agency in the area to really put out a clean product. I hired the hottest video producer in the area, to create a video of the photo shoot. However, as I was forced out of business in 2008, in a depressed state it would be

2011 before Sassy would surface again. I took the concept to a local retail store owner who was thrilled to have it placed in his store. I also, met with the buyers of a major corporate retail chain. They too, were ready to move on a deal. However, I realized that my passion was no longer in that game. After months of negotiating with international manufacturers and, developing production projections for the gear to hit a sample 100 stores, the idea of losing a lot of money again had beat me down.

In between MyHipHopDepartment.com and Sassy Girl Fashions, I created a business called Blue Chip Gamer.com where I conducted onsite and online video game tournaments. Growing up a gamer, this is the one business besides Kamatè that I can say I really enjoyed. It was short lived but, it was fun! I simply created tournaments for gamers to compete at locations and, online for cash prizes.

So, these were some of my primary ventures. However for every one primary venture were three secondary ventures, two ventures that never got off the ground and five ideas that I still have in my shoe box that I have not tapped into yet.

I have come up with some great ideas. However the most fulfilling is truly sharing my story, my song, with you. This is the best idea I ever had right now!